DATE DUE

2 Dec '74		
MAR 1 4 1989		
		PRINTED IN U.S.A.

Columbia University

Contributions to Education

Teachers College Series

No. 427

AMS PRESS

NEW YORK

MORAL EDUCATION AMONG THE NORTH AMERICAN INDIANS

BY

CLAUDE ANDREW NICHOLS, Ph.D.

TEACHERS COLLEGE, COLUMBIA UNIVERSITY
CONTRIBUTIONS TO EDUCATION, No 427

BUREAU OF PUBLICATIONS
Teachers College, Columbia University
NEW YORK CITY
1930

Library of Congress Cataloging in Publication Data

Nichols, Claude Andrew, 1877-
    Moral education among the North American Indians. [New
vi, 104p. 23 cm. (Columbia Univ. York, AMS Press, 1972
    Reprint of the 1930 ed., ~~issued in series~~: Teachers
College, ~~Columbia University~~. Contributions to edu-
cation, no. 427.)
    ~~Originally presented as the author's thesis, Columbia~~.
    Bibliography: p. 101-104.
    1. Indians of North America--Ethics. 2. Indians of
North America--Culture. 3. Indians of North America--
Education. I. Title. II. Series: ~~Columbia University~~
~~Teachers College. Contributions to education, no. 427~~.
E98.E83N5 1972   970.1   75-177112
ISBN 0-404-55427-X

Reprinted by Special Arrangement with Teachers
College Press, New York, New York

From the edition of 1930, New York
First AMS edition published in 1972
Manufactured in the United States

AMS PRESS, INC.
NEW YORK, N. Y.   10003

ACKNOWLEDGMENTS

To Dr. Paul Monroe the author wishes to express his appreciation for many suggestions concerning methods of research. The opinion of Dr. Franz Boas was the deciding factor in the selection of most of the types presented. Dr. Pliny E. Goddard has given the author the advantage of his knowledge and experience in the field by directing him to corroborative sources. Dr. Goddard, Dr. Edward H. Reisner, and Dr. Isaac L. Kandel have made valuable criticisms in the preparation of the manuscript.

C. A. N.

CONTENTS

MORAL EDUCATION AMONG THE NORTH AMERICAN INDIANS

CHAPTER I

INTRODUCTION

In treatises on ethics, in the history of education, and in various forms of educational writings, many references are made to the ideas and practices of primitive man. Some of these references are based on a special study of original source material concerning selected groups, but others go no farther than general works on anthropology. The literature of anthropology contains an abundance of scientific data describing the culture of primitive peoples. However, if one tries to find just what moral ideas the primitive groups in particular areas in many parts of the world taught their children and how they taught them, he is confronted with the task of searching through a large collection of information in which the facts sought appear mingled with data on the numerous other subjects in which the original investigator was often more interested.

In view of these facts, it does not seem out of place to undertake to collect and make easily accessible some of the available historical data concerning the moral ideas which the North American Indians instilled in the individual, and the methods by which their ideas were transmitted. An additional reason for such a contribution lies in the fact that within the last twenty years scientifically trained investigators working among the Indians have gathered a large amount of information that was not utilized by the older works on anthropology.

The older general anthropological treatises based their conclusions concerning moral education largely on the observation of religious forms and conventional morality. They placed little emphasis on the ethical value of public ceremonies. As a result, they concluded that the method of primitive education was, on the whole, blind, unthinking imitation. On the other hand, recent contributions on the culture of the North American Indians show clearly that in ethical morality the individual was taught to think, "to weigh actions and their consequences." Educational agencies consciously stimulated the young to develop moral qualities of individual and social value. To present and interpret the aims, means, and methods of these agencies in their ethical teachings is the purpose of these chapters.

In the interpretation of the life of the American Indians, anthropologists have developed the idea of culture areas. Wissler calls our attention to the universal tendency of mankind to specialize in some particular kind of food to which other sources of food become secondary.[1] The Indian's quest for food and clothing, the methods adopted in his search, and the struggles and conflicts that resulted from it became more potent factors in determining his culture than his physical type or the linguistic stock from which he sprang.[2]

A glance at the accompanying map by Wissler shows the relative positions of the original culture areas in North America. In the eastern half of the United States we find an agricultural area, with maize the principal source of food. In Mexico and Central America agriculture was intensive. Wild game was no longer sufficient to supply any great amount of food. Intensive agriculture developed permanent locations, a more regular food supply, more substantial dwellings, and it made possible an increase in population. Long periods of peace, the accumulation of wealth, and the possibility of leisure time were conditions favorable to intellectual development as well as to the introduction of vices. Evidence of these factors may be seen in the family education of the early Mexicans.

The North Pacific Coast is characterized as the salmon area. Protected by water on one side and by a mountain range on the other, the Tlingit in this territory devoted very little time to warlike pursuits. Their interests centered in the struggle for food and clothing. Distinction was won by the accumulation of property and the generous sharing of food in times of need.

In the Plains Area the people depended almost entirely on the buffalo as a source of food. The hunt often called for long excursions and did not require a permanent home. Such conditions caused conflicts which perpetuated the warlike spirit characterizing the whole life of the Indians who inhabited this region.

[1] Wissler, *The North American Indian*, p. 1.
[2] Wissler, *North American Indians of the Plains*, p. 12.

The influences of the culture area are important in this study because they determine the qualities of character which the tribe admired and endeavored to instill in its members.

With this view of Indian life, how may we get the most ade-- quate conception of moral education among the North American

CULTURE AREAS IN NORTH AMERICA
From Wissler, *North American Indians of the Plains.*

Indians? The plan followed calls for the selection of at least one representative type of each of the main means or agencies that were influential in the transmission of tribal standards and ideals. Corroborative evidence concerning the use of the type in other tribes has been presented to give some idea of the general application of the conclusions reached. One type that has not been included is the special education of the priest, the shaman, or the medicine man. Among many tribes the shaman got his claim to supernatural power through fasting, prayer, and a vision. In some cases, there was a formal initiation into a medicine society, in which a few moral ideas were taught. However, most of the information which the priest, the shaman, or the medicine man received was gained through special paid instructors or through apprenticeship, sometimes for a long period of years. The educational means or agencies, then, that have been chosen are: (1) myths, (2) family and village life, (3) the sun dance and military societies, and (4) a religious ceremony with a distinctly educational purpose.

(1) For a study of the use of stories, Tlingit myths have been taken as a type on account of their large number of stories with moral situations that were applicable in the instruction of the young. They are treated first because they represent a low stage in the organization and unity of thought.

John R. Swanton visited the Tlingit in Alaska, in 1904, for the Bureau of American Ethnology.[3] His information was secured from seven narrators representing six different bands. Two of the men were church members. The only woman from whom he secured data had lived with the whites. Some of his informants, then, had been in contact with the whites or were acquainted with Christian ideas. Nevertheless, Mr. Swanton does not think that these connections affected the stories to any appreciable extent. Further, the stories themselves carry their own internal evidence of primitive origin. When Christian influences appear they are easily detected. The only aspect concerning which some questions might be raised lies in the claims of one of the narrators concerning immediate moral applications with specific purposes. This doubt which will be discussed later does not invalidate the myths as a basis for study.

(2) Concerning family education, systematic statements of the facts are more difficult to find. Five accounts have been selected for brief treatment. The most highly developed type of primitive family education was that of the Aztecs in Mexico. The best record of it is found in Sahagun's *Histoire Générale des Choses de la Nouvelle-Espagne*, translated and edited by Jourdanet and Simeon in 1880. Bernardino de Sahagun reached Mexico in 1529

---

[3] Swanton, *Tlingit Myths and Texts*, p. 1

in a group of twenty Franciscans who were to establish a school
for Mexicans. As he soon acquired some facility in the native
tongue, his superiors directed him to gather facts about the
life and customs of the people. His inquiries led him to the best-
informed men in the region from whom he secured the data which
we have. Greater validity, it seems, is given his work by the fact
that it was originally written in Nahuatl, the language spoken
from the valley of Mexico south to Nicaragua.[4]

In 1896, Earl and Mary S. Barnes published a brief but very
satisfactory discussion of "Education Among the Aztecs." [5] From
Sahagun they translated parts of the discourses of the father and
the mother to their children. Such discourses furnish fairly definite ideas concerning family education.

Two treatises dealing specifically with the education of the
Pueblos have been selected. In 1884, Mrs. Matilde Coxe Stevenson wrote a paper on "The Religious Life of the Zuñi Child"
which was published in the Fifth Annual Report of the Bureau
of American Ethnology. Her husband, an ethnologist, was in
charge of the expedition during which she made her investigations.
Both were initiated into several secret organizations. In 1899,
Frank C. Spencer published *Education of the Pueblo Child* as a
doctor's dissertation in Columbia University. He utilized Mrs.
Stevenson's work and made observations himself among the
Pueblos.

In 1901-02, Frank Russell visited the Pima Indians and later
published an extensive paper in the Seventh Annual Report of
the Bureau of American Ethnology. With headquarters at Saca-
ton, in southwestern Arizona, he had the assistance of five native
interpreters and secured data from ten Pima men and women
especially selected. He made house-to-house visits in the villages
and collected many specimens of Pima art. He included in his
report a brief account of Pima education in the family.

Charles A. Eastman, an educated Sioux, has given in his
Indian Boyhood what he calls "the imperfect record of my boyish
experiences up to the age of fifteen." [6] He is a physician who has
devoted much time to medical work with the Indians, both for the
government and as Indian secretary for the Young Men's Chris-

---

[4] Sahagun, Introduction, Chaps. VII, VIII.
[5] Barnes, *Studies in Education*, Vol. I, pp. 73-80.
[6] Eastman, *Indian Boyhood*, Introduction.

tian Association.[7] He was born at Redwood Falls, Minnesota, in 1858. His work, therefore, covers the period from about 1863 to 1873. One of his reasons for writing the book was to portray for his son the life that he himself had lived. He unquestionably selected the more ideal elements and omitted others that were also characteristic of Indian life. Nevertheless, the incidents which he recounts are unmistakably primitive. His work is especially valuable because it furnishes a type from the Indians of the Plains.

(3) Information on the sun-dance ceremonies and the various societies of the Plains Indians has been collected by the American Museum of Natural History. Beginning in 1907,[8] the staff of the Museum began a systematic survey of the culture of many tribes of the Plains with the result that in 1916 a volume was completed on the societies in this area, and in 1921 there was issued a volume on the sun dance, edited by Clark Wissler.[9] As the references will show, extensive use has been made of data furnished in these papers by Pliny E. Goddard, Robert H. Lowie, Alanson Skinner, Leslie Spier, J. R. Walker, W. D. Wallis, and Clark Wissler. The contributions of George A. Dorsey [10] and A. L. Kroeber [11] have also been helpful.

(4) "Religiousness" was one of the striking characteristics of the North American Indians. Just as war was a constant factor in their thoughts so was religious observance a constant practice in their lives. In daily life, in ceremonies, in the hunt, and in war, they appealed to the supernatural powers for aid. The Hako, as a religious ceremony, represents a high type of appeal and at the same time introduces very effectively many moral teachings. After years of investigation, Miss Alice C. Fletcher, who had been Assistant of Ethnology for the Peabody Museum of American Archaeology and Ethnology since 1882, succeeded in getting a complete description of the sacred objects, the rituals, and their meanings in the Hako. Miss Fletcher served several times as special Indian Agent for the government.

The authorities given include the main sources which have entered into the preparation of the studies which follow.

[7] *Who's Who in America*, Vol. XII, pp. 995-96.

[8] Wissler, Introduction to *Societies of the Plains Indians*, p. 6.

[9] *Societies of the Plains Indians* and *The Dance of the Blackfoot Indians,* *Anthropological Papers, American Museum of Natural History*, Vols. XI and XVI.

[10] Dorsey, *The Cheyenne*, Vol. II, *The Sun Dance*.

[11] Kroeber, *The Arapaho*.

CHAPTER II

TLINGIT EDUCATION

The Tlingit Indians lived along the coast and on the islands of Alaska from Mount St. Elias to the river Nass, with the exception of the southern third of the Prince of Wales Island and small islands to the southwest. Swanton found fourteen geographical groups or tribes. Descent was counted through the mother. The Tlingit recognized two phratries, the Wolf and the Raven. Marriage was not allowed within the phratry. Each phratry included clans which traced their origin to camps that they had occupied. Clans were subdivided into houses or groups, each occupying one or more houses. Thus every geographical group contained representatives of both phratries and several clans.[1]

The Tlingit house group possessed a large house in town and, in addition, a section of territory which included hunting grounds and a salmon creek. Near the latter the members of the group maintained a smokehouse, and in the spring and summer they went there to catch and dry fish and to hunt for game. Sections of the coast from which shellfish were secured, halibut banks, berry patches, and root-digging grounds were owned by many individual clans or families. Some territory was free for all. Those who did not own plots had to seek their food from the common grounds or wait until others had secured what they wanted from their own lands.[2]

The sea and the creeks, then, were the principal sources of food for the Tlingit. It may be noted that the process of obtaining a food supply from the sea or by digging and berrying was not as exciting nor as fascinating as was the hunt of the Indians of the Plains. The Tlingit therefore developed the ideal of work for the man as well as for the woman.

The Tlingit naturally controlled the trade between the coast and

[1] Swanton, *Social Condition, Beliefs, and Linguistic Relationships of the Tlingit Indians*, pp. 396-407.
[2] *Ibid.*, p. 425.

7

the inland tribes. Protected on the one side by the sea and on the other by mountains, they were not in such constant danger of attack as were the Plains Indians. Their stories reflect this situation by devoting very little attention to warlike deeds. They sometimes went on distant military expeditions largely for the purpose of capturing slaves which they brought home to serve them. The fact that they went some distance on these expeditions shows that fighting was not as common an activity as it was in some other parts of the continent. Their petty warfare was most frequently undertaken to avenge the death of a clansman.

They had large, strong houses built of cedar in which several families sometimes lived together. Members of these groups also worked together in securing food and supplies. Such relations help to explain the emphasis that they place on the story as a means of teaching. They may also help us to understand their strong feeling of obligation to the clan. If, in contests, a member of one clan killed a member of another and escaped, the members of the clan of the murdered man demanded the life of a man of equal rank in the clan of the murderer, in case the murderer himself ranked lower than the man whom they had lost. At a meeting, the members of the offended group decided on the man whom they wanted. If his group considered him of the rank of the murdered man, he left them and went out to be killed. The clan of the murderer then punished him by taking his property.[3]

The settlement of such conflicts suggests the Tlingit form of social control. Their stories recognized chiefs who were probably heads of families. They recognized social classes as high-caste and low-caste. High-caste presumed rank by birth, wealth, and certain moral characteristics. Those who lacked these qualities were considered low-caste. However, one might be elevated by noble achievement or wealth, and a man of the higher rank might be considered low-caste on account of his behavior. The individual secured his rights through loyalty to a more or less democratic group held together by blood ties. According to one informant, a man showed his respect for the opposite phratry by selecting his wife from it.[4] He showed his respect for the men of the opposite group by asking them to help him in various ways. Evidently a fairly cordial feeling prevailed.

[3] Swanton, *Social Conditions, Beliefs, and Linguistic Relationships of the Tlingit Indians,* p. 449.
[4] *Ibid.*, p.424.

It is difficult to state the religious beliefs of the Tlingit. They looked upon everything as containing one principal spirit and several subordinates. Hence they opposed disrespectful language toward any object or animal. They gave Raven credit for making the sun, the moon, the stars, rivers and creeks, and for creating people, but their stories imply the existence of human beings before such acts of creation were accomplished.[5] The stories do not indicate that they worshiped Raven. He is more frequently portrayed as an ever-hungry, lazy trickster, scheming to get possession of food without work. The indefinite nature of their religious ideas will be seen from a consideration of their teachings.

Aims and Methods of Teaching

An effort to discover and describe the means, methods, and purposes of moral education as they appear in the folklore of a people has little to do with those aspects of training by which the individual learns to carry on the ordinary activities of life. The acquisition of skills is frequently presented but it is nearly always explained by mythical connections. The main interests of folklore lie in the realm of achievement, thought, attitudes, and social values. It is a record of man's effort to rationalize his experience and to set up standards by which conduct may be guided. The legend proves satisfying through its relations to permanent social needs and values, and these are worked into moral purposes and standards.

The accumulated intellectual possessions of the Tlingit Indians cover various fields of thought. The origin of clan emblems, names, and many social customs, the potency of medicines and charms, the practice of shamanism and witchcraft, the spirit world, and a more or less fragmentary cosmology appear over and over in their myths. However, as selection is necessary, some idea of their view of the world will be presented, and then attention will be limited largely to those stories which have a more or less close relation to morals.

The great mythical character of the Tlingit was the Raven. He was spoken of as a bird that had superior power by which he could transform himself into man or beast or by which he could at least keep his identity unknown for a time. A large number of

[5] Swanton, *Tlingit Myths and Texts*, pp. 3, 4, 18, 19.

the stories center around him. He appears in the first myth of
the collection as a maker of the world. Although Raven's father
had given him strength to make the world, he had to resort to
crafty schemes in order to accomplish his purposes. Realizing
that light was needed, he conceived plans by which he might get
it from a rich man who kept it in his house far up the River Nass.
He made himself into a very small piece of dirt and dropped into
the water. The rich man's daughter swallowed him, and later he
was born her child. As the child crawled about in the house, he
cried continually for some bundles that were hanging on the wall.
His grandfather gave him one of them. After playing with it for
a time, the child let it go up through the smoke-hole into the sky.
It was a bag containing the stars which scattered and took their
places as we see them now. In a similar way he secured the moon.
The last thing that he cried for was a box containing the daylight,
which his grandfather was reluctant to give up. With this box
he flew out, uttering the raven's cry "Ga." He drank up the fresh
water of a spring by deceiving the owner Petrel from whom he
escaped only after Petrel's smoke-hole spirits had held him long
enough for the smoke to turn his feathers black. By spitting out
the water which he still held, he made the Nass, the Stikine, the
Taku, and other rivers while, with small drops, he made the creeks.
On reaching a large town where the people who had never seen
daylight were catching eulachon, he requested them to take him
to the opposite bank. When they refused and showed a disposition
to quarrel, he opened his box of daylight from which the sun flew
to the sky. The people there in the sunlight became the animals
whose skins they wore.[6]

In this peculiarly naïve and uncritical way the narrative of
Raven's experiences continues. Although he appeared at one
place as a person, at another as a bird, at another as the companion
of various animals, his kaleidoscopic transformations and marvelous achievements do not seem to have suggested questions of
possibility, or the need of any explanation whatever. In the
course of his wandering and rather irregular life, he continued to
have influence with natural forces and was given credit for teaching men the use of certain things in hunting, fishing, and ordinary
activities. Many explanations of the origin of physical characteristics and habits of animals are attributed to him.

[6] Swanton, *Tlingit Myths and Texts*, pp. 3-5.

As we leave cosmological conceptions and reach Raven's experiences with human beings, though miraculous performances continue, there is some recognition of rational connections and of moral situations. Tlingit life did not stop with securing and enjoying the bare necessities. Although the struggle for existence was severe, the Tlingit mind was at work bringing almost all aspects of experience into the realm of thought. When Raven schemed for the improvement of human conditions, his acts were related in such a way that they must have received approval. When he assumed the rôle of an individual in conflict with the interests and needs of the group, his conduct was frequently cited as an example of what should be avoided. These social relations and conflicts form the basis for the consciously directed education of the Tlingit; their myths give the starting point for instruction.

The moral ideas concerning high-caste and low-caste, honesty, kindness and generosity, work, bravery, conjugal affection, respectful language and conduct, conduct of girls, social welfare, and the spirit world appear repeatedly in the literature of the Indians. With many of these we have also the narrator's comment as to how each episode was used to teach certain ideas to the young.

These ideas were evidently taught after the child was old enough to follow simple reasoning. The Tlingit had two stories which they told to children in order to keep them from crying. In one, a child kept crying from hunger until Man-with-a-burning-hand called him and promised him food. He took him away and gave him ants to eat. The child's parents went out to search for the child. Guided by his cry, they lifted a rock near a cliff and found his body covered with ants. Many children were brought to the place and told that such would be their fate if they cried.[7] In the other story, the father of a crying boy called out for a man who had been captured by the land otters to get the boy. A land-otter-man came and took the boy away. He fed him on what appeared to be blackberries. After two days the parents began to look for the boy. They found him far up in the woods. He was filled with spiders which his father and mother saw come out of him leaving nothing but the skin. It can hardly be doubted that these stories were told effectively.

High-Caste. High-caste among the Tlingit implied a standard of wealth and a standard of morality as well. One of the Raven

[7] *Ibid.*, p. 145. (Told at Wrangell).

myths relates how an old low-caste man, Damnadji, deceived a high-caste girl and married her. A graphic picture of her disappointment is given. Her husband's neighbors made fun of him for marrying out of his rank. The most humiliating scene, however, was the visit and disappointment of the girl's father and brothers. Yet when they learned the truth, they did not make fun of the old man. He was transformed, by magic, into a man of wealth. However, the old man in his prosperity was hard upon his people. Later he lost both his wife and his wealth. Swanton's informant tells how this story was used for two purposes: to teach a young man to marry in his own rank, and to show the conduct becoming for the high-caste. The troubles of the old man were told in order to show the unhappy situations that would come upon those who followed his example. The story was also used to teach young men to save up a considerable sum before marrying, so that they would not be the object of ridicule of the group.

The refusal of the girl's relatives to make fun of her husband was presented as proof of the fact that they were really high-caste. Her brothers had too much respect for their sister to contribute to the disgrace of her husband even though he deserved their scorn. The pride of Damnadji in his prosperity was given as one reason why his money left him.[8]

A Raven myth recorded at Wrangell begins with the observation that in olden times only high-caste people had sufficient time to learn the story of Raven properly.[9] In another story in which the evils of gambling were set forth, we are informed that high-caste people taught their children that gambling had its place among lower people and was not proper for an honest person.[10]

In these instances, knowledge and principles of conduct seem to be implied in the idea of high-caste. Such a conclusion is further justified by the fact that individuals of low birth who possessed certain attainments and principles were ranked as high-caste. A similar conception is found in our use of the word "gentleman" to designate a high standard of conduct.

Honesty. The Tlingit were very definite in their disapproval of selfish impulses and acquisitive methods that went beyond the actual needs of the individual. Greed, nearly always linked with

[8] Swanton, *Tlingit Myths and Texts*, pp. 109-14.
[9] *Ibid.*, p. 80.
[10] *Ibid.*, pp. 138-39.

deception, received definite condemnation. In spite of his many good qualities, Raven is cited as the example not to be followed.

In one of the Wrangell myths a story is told of how Raven flew into the mouth of a whale, cut out its heart, and killed it. From within he shouted that the one who would cut open the whale would be considered high-born. When the people gathered around the whale and cut it open, Raven flew into the woods, with the cry, Q!oné, q!oné, q!oné. After some time he returned and was apparently surprised to find numerous boxes of whale grease. In answer to his questions the people told how it happened. To his inquiry whether they heard anything inside the whale, they replied that something flew out giving a cry. Thereupon, he warned them that years before in another town such a thing happened and caused all the people to die. Following Raven's advice and alarmed by his tale, the people left their boxes of grease which he promptly appropriated.[11]

After relating this story in detail the narrator added:

In our days when a person is making a living dishonestly by lying and stealing, he is not told so directly; but this story is brought up to him, and everyone knows what it means.

In order to teach children not to be greedy and selfish, or in order to shame some person who was selfish in a trade, the following story was told: "On coming upon some children who were throwing pieces of fat at each other in play, Raven made himself look like a child and joined in the sport. As pieces of fat came his way he promptly ate them. The children of course soon raised the question as to where their fat was going." Parents would thus urge their children not to be like Raven "who ate up all his playmates' fat." People would remind the greedy person that he wanted to enjoy everything himself.[12]

In the Tlingit teachings against stealing, religious mystery was introduced undoubtedly to add to the effect. Raven, in his wanderings, came to a large house in town where everyone seemed to have died. As he entered the house he could see nobody, but he felt someone pushing against him. He filled a canoe with the provisions which he found. As he started away a rope pulled the canoe back to the shore, while invisible hands carried the stolen property back to the house. A stone dropped upon the Raven's

[11] *Ibid.*, pp. 91-92.
[12] *Ibid.*, p. 92.

foot and made him lame. He had stolen the goods from the ghost house in the Town of Ghosts. The narrator gives a detailed explanation of the use of this story:

> This episode is brought up to a child people desire to make honest. They say that just as these goods were taken back from Raven, and he was made to feel shame at having been discovered, a thief will always be found out. If a child becomes a thief when he grows up, they tell him that he will be classed among the very lowest, no matter how well born he was. They also tell the little ones that there is a Creator watching them all the time, just as these ghosts watched. The Raven could not see them, but they saw him. They say that a person who does evil things is like a crippled or deformed person, for he has disgraced his family. They tell them that a person who gets that low is nobody, and that the Creator despises him.[13]

The negative aspect of the instruction concerning honesty calls for explanation. It is quite probable that the positive elements were not often clearly in the Tlingit consciousness. So long as everyone was honest there was no conflict of interests, no special problem or crisis. When someone attempted to appropriate more than his share or to secure his share improperly, the moral issue was forced on the minds of the members of the group. On such occasions the instruction was given. Honesty, to the Tlingit mind, meant repression of selfish impulses.

Kindness and Generosity. In the story of Djiyin, kindness to orphans, to the homeless, and even to those who have harmed one was taught. During a famine, an orphan girl accompanied her aunt and other women who were searching for roots. As the girl was not to be found when they were ready to return, the women, after throwing water on the fire, started to go without her. The girl's aunt, however, slipped back to save some coals and dried salmon for her. On seeing her aunt, the girl told her that she was going to remain there because the others did not want to take her. In a short time she became a shaman. Although the people of her village had treated her very cruelly, she was not only ready to give them plenty to eat when they were in need but was also willing to heal their sick. Her greatest favors, however, were reserved for her aunt who had been kind to her and for two orphan girls who had received unkind treatment from their people. These were honored more than the high-caste of the group.[14]

[13] Swanton, *Tlingit Myths and Texts*, p. 92. The term "Creator" suggests Christian influences. The rest of the story is undoubtedly primitive.
[14] *Ibid.*, pp. 182-84.

In the story, "The Man Fed from the Sky," a young man who seemed to be worthless was treated more or less unkindly except by one of the two wives of his uncle, the chief, in whose house he lived. By some magic power he secured a large quantity of food in a period of great want. Although he had reason to be hostile toward the people of the village, he generously shared his provisions with them. His uncle, the chief, after praising him for his liberal attitude, offered to give him one of his wives. The young man selected the one who had always been kind to him; and his kindness to the people continued after he had become very wealthy.[15]

The myths contain many similar instances in which good was returned for evil, while kindness was usually singled out to receive the greatest reward.

Work. The Tlingit used a number of stories to show their disrespect for the man who did not work. In order to get across a stream, Raven requested some men who were in a canoe fishing for halibut to carry him to the other bank. As they paid no attention to him, he held out his walking stick; and the story goes thus: "And they found themselves going up into the sky. They are seen there now as the 'halibut-fishers.'" According to the narrator, "when a child was lazy and disobedient, they told him how the halibut fishermen got up into the sky for their laziness. Therefore the children were afraid of being lazy." [16]

In another story Raven figured as the example of laziness. He went to the house of a fish hawk who had gathered an abundant supply of food for the winter. Delighted with such surroundings, Raven decided to spend the entire season with his new friend. However, his refusal to work soon exasperated his host, who was not satisfied with Raven's assurances of his high rank and of his willingness to work later. He finally determined to abandon Raven and leave him to shift for himself. The narrator makes the following application of this story:

This is the way nowadays with persons who have no respect for themselves. They go from house to house to be fed by others, and such persons are greedy, great eaters, and lazy. The people tell their children that those who lead this kind of life are not respected. When Katishan was a boy, they used to say to him when they could not make him do anything, "You are so lazy that you will be left in some village alone." (It is said that

[15] *Ibid.*, pp. 189-92.
[16] *Ibid.*, p. 107.

Raven comes along and helps one abandoned in a village.) This is why the Tlingit tried hard to earn their living and make things comfortable for themselves.[17]

After this experience Raven went to visit an industrious fishing bird whom he called his brother-in-law. The bird received him kindly but left him the next day "for he knew he was a lazy fellow."

So it is always said, "A lazy fellow will be known wherever he goes." Such a person will go from place to place living on others and perhaps bringing in a few pails of water or some wood for his food; but, however high-caste he is, he will be looked down upon. Therefore the little ones were taught to stay in their native place and make their living there, instead of wandering from town to town. To this day, the high-caste Indians do so and visit in other towns only for a short time. Then people say, "Look at so-and-so. He stays in his own village.[18]

Bravery. The Tlingit have few stories relating to warfare. Their great struggles were with wild animals and the forces of nature. Personal bravery in battle does not seem to have been idealized. The struggle with the animal world and the unseen powers appears repeatedly in their myths. In "The Salmon Chief," a fisherman had two sons; one was very brave but the other, who stayed at home, was called a coward. The brave boy once came to a place where the people were going to give the chief's daughter to a seven-headed monster in order to keep it from murdering everyone in the village. He ran alone to the monster's den before which the girl had been left. After a hard fight he cut off the monster's head to the great joy of the people who had been living in terror. The story relates approvingly the pride of the father and the marriage of the boy to the chief's daughter in spite of the poverty of his parents.[19]

In the story, "The Youthful Warrior," bravery in battle is introduced but the acts described are largely matters of personal revenge combined with the use of magic and the spirit world.[20]

In the account of "The First War in the World," there are fragmentary stories of expeditions to the south and to the north for purposes of retaliation, although no permanent heroes are especially singled out. People going to war tried to get the spirit

---

[17] Swanton, *Tlingit Myths and Texts,* p. 117.
[18] *Ibid.,* p. 117.
[19] *Ibid.,* pp. 196-98.
[20] *Ibid.,* pp. 69-71.

of a certain man who was swallowed by a devilfish in a fight in which he killed the monster.[21] Finally the northern warriors went south in a big canoe on a journey of probably ten days. They killed or captured nearly all of the people. "Since that time people have been freer to camp where they please." [22]

Family Relations. Respect and protection for motherhood are clearly taught in several stories. "The Man Who Married the Eagle," after killing a man involved in his wife's infidelity and escaping from the village, finally gained magic power by marrying the daughter of an eagle. By means of this power he provided for his mother's needs. On one occasion men of the town insolently struck her with a rock. The eagle seized the chief by the head and lifted him from the ground. Then he brought the chief low enough to enable another man to catch his legs which he could not let go. This movement was repeated until all the men were carried away together.[23]

Kindness to the mother-in-law was expected of the wife. In "The Origin of the Screech Owl," an account is given of how a woman gave her mother-in-law a hot rock instead of some fish. Later on, when her husband had brought in a canoe load of herring, she called to the people to bring down her basket so that she could carry up the fish. They heard her but, because of her conduct, paid no attention to her. As she shouted louder and louder, her voice changed until she began hooting like an owl. At length her calls for her basket ceased; the hooting alone continued for she had become the screech owl.

Nowadays, when a young girl is very selfish, people say to her, "Ah! when you get married, you will put a hot rock into your mother-in-law's hands, and for punishment will become an owl." [24]

The treatment that men were expected to give their wives is shown in several stories selected as incidents from longer myths. When Raven, in a quarrel with his wife, the daughter of Fog-over-the-salmon, struck her with a piece of dried salmon, she ran away from him and would not return. Her father refused to make her go back on the ground that Raven did not respect her and would not take care of her. In regard to the use of this story the narrator says:

[21] *Ibid.*, p. 72.
[22] *Ibid.*, p. 79.
[23] *Ibid.*, pp. 203-06.
[24] *Ibid.*, pp. 176-77, 299.

When a young man was about to marry, people would bring this story up to him and tell him that if he did not take care of his wife and once forgot himself, he might lose her. If his wife were a good woman and he treated her right, he would have money and property; but if he were mean to her, he would lose it. And if he lost his wife and had not been good to her, he could not get another easily.[25]

In the story of "Little Felon," a young man by performing several marvelous feats won a beautiful girl with whom he lived happily for a time. Later, however, there was a quarrel which brought on cruel treatment from the young husband. The woman, after leaving him and sitting down on a promontory, disappeared. In spite of his searches he could find no trace of her. "He is a lonely beach snipe, which is often seen hunting about on points to-day; and when the Tlingit see him they say, 'There he is, looking for his wife.' "[26]

In "The Image That Came to Life," the story is told of a young chief who had an image made of his dead wife. After he had dressed the image in his wife's marten-skin robe, he felt that she had returned to him. He ate with the image close at hand; he mourned near it and hoped that it would come to life.[27]

In the story, "The Returned from Spirit Land," a high-caste young man, whose wife died shortly after their marriage, could not sleep for two nights. The morning following the second night he put on his best clothes and left home. He walked all day and all night along the death road to the shore of a lake. He was finally carried across and then brought his wife back in the ghost's canoe. She was a shadow which followed him wherever he went. She kept quiet during the day but all night long the two could be heard playing together. When a jealous suitor of the woman interfered one night, a rattling of bones was heard. "That instant the woman's husband died, and the ghosts of both of them went back to Ghost Land." The permanence of affection could hardly be portrayed more vividly to the savage mind.[28]

Respectful Language and Conduct. As two high-caste boys were going out to play one night, one of them made the remark that the moon was about the shape and size of his mother's labret. His companion warned him that he should not speak of the moon

[25] Swanton, *Tlingit Myths and Texts*, p. 108.
[26] *Ibid.*, pp. 177-80.
[27] *Ibid.*, p. 181.
[28] *Ibid.*, pp. 249-50.

in that way. In punishment for his disrespectful language, the boy was carried up to the moon from which he escaped with great difficulty.[29]

A high-caste girl made a disrespectful remark concerning a snail. She was carried off and married to the snail the next evening. The story continues with the fact that, although she was rescued by her brothers, they considered themselves disgraced. In many stories, scornful treatment was followed by some disaster to the guilty person or to his group. A certain degree of respect was considered due not only to people but also to animals and things.

Conduct of Girls. At the beginning of puberty girls were forbidden to look at anyone for a long time. In one of the Raven stories, a girl's brothers were crossing a stream, and the mother said she thought that they had fallen into the water; the girl, in her anxiety looked out at them, and they were turned into stone. Mothers told this story to girls in the beginning of adolescence. They were urged to be obedient to their mothers and respectful to their brothers. The fate of the boys was used as a warning.

Girls were taught to observe certain other restraints in conduct when they were approaching maturity. One of the Raven myths gave concrete basis for the teaching. Raven undertook to pass the six months of winter in the ground hog's house. Although the ground hog enjoyed himself very much, Raven soon became sick of the situation but could not get out. Believing that the ground hog had power to make the winter pass, Raven kept shouting, "Winter comes on." Finally he pulled off one of the ground hog's six toes from each foot in a vain effort to shorten the winter.

This episode used to be brought up to girls fourteen and fifteen who wanted to run about to feasts and other festivities without their mothers or grandmothers. Such girls were told that they were like Raven when he was imprisoned in the ground hog hole and wanted to get out. Those who stayed indoors were respected by everybody. They also likened Raven to a foolish girl who tries to lead a good girl, Ground hog, astray. They told the latter that some injury would result, as happened to Ground hog in losing his toes. When a mother saw that her daughter was willing to listen to a foolish girl, she would say to her, "Whatever that foolish girl leads you to will be seen on you as long as you live." [30]

Social Welfare. The idea that the individual should consider the welfare of the group is clearly shown in several of the stories

[29] *Ibid.,* pp. 209-12.
[30] *Ibid.,* p. 108.

already quoted. The selling of private property in times of need was mentioned with approval. The free distribution of food, however, was more highly esteemed.

One of the myths tells how the Wolverine-man taught a hunter to catch animals with traps. The latter was very successful and divided the skins with his friends. He became very wealthy from renting his trap to others so that they could secure their food and clothing.[31]

In the story of the Wolf Chief's son, an ideal of service to the group is portrayed without any comments. In a time of famine many people of the town died for want of food. A young boy who was always hunting found a small animal that looked like a dog. He put it under his blanket and carried it home to care for it. He painted its head and legs so that he could trace it while hunting. It brought him birds, mountain sheep, and other animals. The boy thus provided well for his parents and friends. When he killed game he always gave the best of it to the dog. With some reluctance he lent the dog to his sister's husband who, instead of giving it the best, threw at it the entrails of a mountain sheep. After this treatment the dog ran away. The boy was very sad when he heard the news and set out immediately to seek the dog's trail. Following the directions of an old woman he reached the town of the wolves. The little dog was the Wolf Chief's son who had sent him to help the people in their distress. The boy stayed in the town of the wolves two nights, so he thought, but really he remained nearly two years. The Wolf Chief was kind to him and gave him a magic quill by means of which he could kill animals or heal the sick. The boy returned home with his quill and found all the people dead. He restored them to life and provided food. He became wealthy from presents given him for healing the sick.[32]

While the informant made no moral applications in connection with these stories, the implied approval of the type of social conduct described was quite clear.

The Spirit World. The belief that birds, animals, and various objects had spirits that participated in the affairs of men appears over and over in Tlingit traditions. Many of the stories to which references have been made clearly imply a belief in animism with-

[31] Swanton, *Tlingit Myths and Texts*, pp. 36-38.
[32] *Ibid.*, pp. 33-36.

out any apparent intent to teach it as such. Control over the spirits of birds and animals or coöperation with them was the great source of magic power for shamans or medicine men.

Though more or less vague and ill-defined, there was a belief in life after death. The corpse was burned so that the spirit of the deceased might remain near the fire in the ghosts' home. Otherwise, the spirit of the deceased would have to stay far back in the house and shake, regardless of the number of blankets that it had.[33] In the story of the Alsek River people, a brave man's body was not burned because brave men did not want to sit like weaklings near the fire in the ghosts' home.[34] In memorial ceremonies, property and food were sometimes burned so that they might be available for the dead.[35]

The Tlingit did not seem to relate moral conduct to future life or, to any great extent, to their religious beliefs. Their taboos and their conventional methods of procedure were based on the supposed presence of spirits and the workings of magic. What we would call social morality was given a rational setting. One informant stated that they formerly worshiped Raven, but the stories as a whole do not indicate this. There was little organization to their thought or forms of worship except in ceremonies in honor of the dead. At a tobacco feast, the speaker insisted that the dead were alive.[36] At the erection of a memorial pole, a chief recited the success of Raven in getting daylight from his grandfather on the Nass and gave this glimpse of ancestor worship:

At that time, his grandchild brought daylight out upon the poor people he had made in the world. He pitied them. This is the way with me. Darkness is upon me. My mind is sick. Therefore I am now begging daylight from you, my grandfathers, my father's brothers, people I came from, my ancestors, my mother's grandfathers. Can it be that you will give the daylight to me as Raven-at-the-head-of-Nass gave it to his grandchild, so that day will dawn upon me?[37]

The Use of Myths in Teaching Morals

The intentional presentation of moral situations in myths and stories was not limited to the Tlingit. Dorsey recognizes the fact

[33] Swanton, *Social Conditions, Beliefs, and Linguistic Relationships of the Tlingit Indians*, p. 425.
[34] Swanton, *Tlingit Myths and Texts*, p. 68.
[35] *Ibid.*, p. 82.
[36] *Ibid.*, p. 372.
[37] *Ibid.*, p. 374.

that some of the Pawnee myths must have been told with a moral purpose. In the story of "The Poor Boy Who Married the Chief's Daughter," bravery for social good was honored.[38] "The Boy Who Was Given Power to Call the Buffalo" and the stories following it were clearly organized to teach certain qualities.[39] In the chapter on the Hako it will be seen that the Pawnee gathered and used stories of birds to convey moral ideas. Grinnell shows many moral situations in his Pawnee stories.[40] The story of "The Deceived Blind Man and the Deserted Children" and other Arapaho traditions have very definite moral values.[41] In the study of family and village education, evidence will be given concerning the teaching of morals through stories by the Santee Sioux, the Pima, and the Pueblos.

If we accept Kroeber's thesis [42] in which he maintains that the Indians of the Northwest represented the lowest stratum of American culture without the general diffusion of traits that took place elsewhere, we have a basis for considering the moral ideas of the Tlingit as representative of a local development of the ideas with which life began in America. Their conceptions of high-caste and low-caste, honesty, kindness and generosity, work, bravery, conjugal affection, the conduct of girls, their attitude of respect toward everything, their obligation to the group and their view of the spirit world were all developments possible in small groups. The absence of constant pressure from the outside accounts for their lack of both political ideas and political forms. Their morality was limited largely to the small group, and within that group individual motives were often given as reasons why a certain line of conduct should be followed. The fact that the Tlingit sometimes abandoned undesirable individuals or punished those who disregarded their customs rather suggests that members, even in their loyalty to the group, were more or less prompted by selfish ends.

Several families living in one house as an economic unit would explain their idea of the importance of work and their teachings against greed. Their struggle for food was hard. Stories about famine show that the specter of actual want rose frequently before their minds. Swanton states that an unwritten law required every

[38] Dorsey, *The Pawnee: Mythology*, pp. 68-71.
[39] *Ibid.*, pp. 90-95.
[40] Grinnell, *Pawnee Hero Stories and Folk Tales*, pp. 45-47
[41] Dorsey and Kroeber, *Traditions of the Arapaho*, pp. 286-93.
[42] Kroeber, *American Culture and the Northwest Coast*, pp. 7-8.

Tlingit to house and feed any member of his phratry who might appear. The Raven stories show that visiting was common. Raven was frequently pictured as a kind of ubiquitous, hungry individual trying to secure food without labor. All of these factors no doubt contributed to help the Tlingit rationalize the importance of honest effort in providing for one's needs.

Swanton also mentions the fact that some were dishonest and used deception in an effort to gain their ends.[43] That the Tlingit were conscious of this weakness is shown by the number of stories in which Raven schemed as a trickster in order to secure food. It is highly possible that their control of trade for the inland tribes increased their inclination to cheat. They did not feel many obligations to the outsider; and, once developed, dishonest methods of dealing were easily applied in the treatment of adjoining groups.

Kroeber's statement that the Indians of the Northwest knew a status of influence without a constituted authority [44] agrees entirely with the implications of the stories. High-caste was maintained by wealth and a high standard of conduct. Even achievement alone could give one high-caste standing. Gambling was considered by some to be unworthy of the high-caste. To make an extended visit was considered a mark of low-caste. In other words, the individual's possessions were not entirely sufficient to give him high social rank. His personality and achievements were also considered.

Apparently their greatest heroes were those who had won in fights with beasts or monsters or who had secured by magic the means of furnishing food for the group. Such factors, rather than war with other tribes, were the dominating influences in Tlingit thought.

Concerning their methods of transmitting moral ideas, there can be no doubt that the stories told on many occasions were without a specific moral purpose. Nevertheless, it seems certain that many of the myths were recounted when the corresponding moral problem was in the foreground. The informant who especially showed this tendency was a church member. However, the practice itself is primitive. As we shall see in the next chapter, the tendency to moralize was quite general. Furthermore, if the story were used consciously for teaching, the most natural thing would be to give it when a vital problem had to be solved. It

[43] Swanton, *Tlingit Myths and Texts*, p. 428.
[44] Kroeber, *op. cit.*, p. 9.

should also be recalled that the Tlingit had two stories which they told to children whom they wished to keep from crying.[45]   There are numerous evidences to show that in many tribes families followed the custom of giving special advice at the time of marriage.[46]

Social approval was their most effective means for securing compliance with their standards.   It required the coöperation of a group to secure food.   To be left alone suggested horrible results. The individual's own wants, therefore, prompted him to live harmoniously with his people.   There can be no doubt that, through myth and story told to the individual or in the house group, a definite effort was made to regulate the social conduct of both the young and the old.

[45] Swanton, *Tlingit Myths and Texts*, pp. 40, 145.
[46] These facts will also appear in the next chapter.

CHAPTER III

FAMILY AND VILLAGE EDUCATION

It is difficult, and by no means necessary, to treat family education apart from the influences of the group that made up the Indian village or camp. In most cases families lived close together for purposes of mutual protection. Sometimes what we would call several families lived in one house or lodge. Though, in a few instances, we are able to find records of the part played by the parents in the education of the child, the activities of the village group were undoubtedly making constant incidental contributions toward the formation of character and the determination of conduct. Frequently a relative, a godfather, a story-teller, or a master took a prominent part in giving the child special instruction.

Somewhat detailed accounts from four different groups have been chosen for the study of family education. These groups are the Aztec in the Mexico and Central America Area, the Pueblo and the Pima in the Southwest Area, and the Santee Sioux in the upper part of the Plains Area. The first three lie in the region of intensive agriculture; the last belongs to the land of the buffalo.

AZTEC EDUCATION

The Aztecs whom the Spaniards found in control of Central Mexico had a civilization highly developed in many respects. They were a conquering nation, having gained control over people of greater culture than they themselves had possessed. They counted their history as a great people from the rule of their first war chief in 1376.[1] In a league with some of their neighbors they were able to maintain their position through their military prowess. Cities with large temples, highly [2] developed religious forms, and no little wealth and material culture were in evidence when the Spaniards conquered the country.

[1] Spinden *Ancient Civilization of Mexico and Central America*, p. 187.
[2] *Ibid.*, pp. 191-93.

25

The education of the Aztecs was described by Sahagun in the sixteenth century within about twenty-five years after the conquest. His report, therefore, should represent their practices before they were influenced by Europeans.

In a spirit of religious devotion some Aztec mothers dedicated their daughters to the service of the temple. When the girls were from twenty to forty days old, the mothers presented them in the temple and made offerings. After that the priest repeatedly urged each mother to educate her daughter well and to continue to make offerings. When the child was old enough to understand her mother's vow, she went to the temple where, under the direction of matrons, she lived until someone asked for her in marriage.[3]

In a similar manner a building somewhat like a monastery was provided for the education of boys of the nobility who were preparing to devote themselves to the service of certain deities.[4] Sahagun said that their fathers gave as reasons that in

... the *calmecac* there were good manners, principles, and practices and a rude and chaste life without anything shameful or reprehensible.[5]

The kings and nobles had both governesses and pages to look after the morals of their children. Under their protection the children went out to play. Mothers cautioned these preceptors not to permit any rudeness, obscenity, or disrespect to anyone, and prescribed forms by which the children should salute their elders.

At the age of ten, boys from these families were sent to a boarding school where they were taught to tell the truth and to practice austerity. Their training involved such menial service as gathering wood, sweeping, making fires, etc.[6] At fifteen, military instruction was begun, and at twenty the boys were taken on a campaign under the particular care of trusted warriors who both instructed and protected them.[7]

The act of entrusting a boy to a teacher at the boarding school or to a warrior created the occasion for discourses. In one of these speeches a master, after asserting that he could not predict what the boy would become, said:

We shall do, then, that which is our duty; we shall educate him, we shall instruct him as his father and mother; but we certainly cannot pene-

[3] Sahagun, *Histoire Générale des Choses de la Nouvelle-Espagne*, pp. 196-97.
[4] *Ibid.*, p. 174.
[5] *Ibid.*, p. 231
[6] *Ibid.*, p. 228.
[7] *Ibid.*, pp. 538-39.

trate his interior and put in him our heart; you who are his parents could not do it yourselves.[8]

Among other things the master said that the boys should not be kept at home and taught a woman's occupation but should learn practices that would tend to make valorous men of them. In some of these establishments drunkenness was punished with death. Some of the pupils had concubines, but such boys were not regarded as leading an exemplary life.[9]

While establishments similar to the boarding school were not unknown among other North American Indians, that which best represents primitive life among the Aztecs was the discourse pronounced by parents when their children reached the age of discretion.

The lord or king was accustomed to address a lecture to his children when they reached the age of reason. He began with an expression of his misgivings in regard to their attitudes, stating his fear that no one of them would be worthy of the dignity and lordship which he possessed.[10] He urged them to worship the gods properly:

Know that those who weep, mourn, sigh, pray, and meditate, and those who voluntarily and of their own accord stay awake at night, and get up early to sweep the streets and the roads, to clean the houses, to arrange the mats and the seats, and prepare the places where God receives sacrifices and offerings, without forgetting to praise the gods early . . . , those who do this hold themselves in the presence of God, become his friends, and obtain his favors.[11]

He told them to be humble and recognize that everything came as a gift from God.

The king's advice, however, was not limited to religion. The following shows his attention to other matters:

Endeavor to know some honorable trade like that of making objects of feathers, or some other mechanical art; for these things can serve to gain subsistence in moments of need.

Direct your attention especially towards that which concerns agriculture, seeing that the earth produces all things, without asking for anything to drink or eat, being sufficient in itself to make them appear. Your predecessors took care to know and to do these things; for, although they were lords and nobles, they did not neglect having their heritage worked and

[8] *Ibid.*, p. 228.
[9] *Ibid.*, p. 230.
[10] *Ibid.*, p. 380.
[11] *Ibid.*, p. 381.

cultivated, and they informed us that their forefathers did likewise. If you applied yourselves only to caring for your rank and nobility without attention to the above things, especially agriculture, with what would you nourish the people of your house? And with what would you entertain yourselves? I have nowhere seen that anyone could nourish himself on his nobility and lofty birth. It behooves you solely to direct your attention to the things necessary for the body like the means of subsistence, for they are the basis of our life.[12]

He closed his lecture by advising them to be the friends of God, humble in heart, respectful toward everybody, and not to waste the time which God had placed at their disposal.[13]

In another discourse, the son was urged to imitate the humility, the dignity, and the grave bearing of his noble ancestors:

Know well, my son, that never has a proud, vain, presumptuous, noisy fellow been elected king. No man, discourteous, ill-bred, foul-mouthed, impertinent in his speech, who says everything that comes to his mind has ever been elevated to the royal rank and throne . . . . Those who in times past directed the state and the armies were all people given to prayer, devotion and sighs, very humble and obedient, and endowed with a quiet and tranquil character.[14]

Sahagun recorded several similar speeches nearly all of which followed more or less the same line of thought.

In discourses to their daughters the lords emphasized the abundance of misery, poverty, labor, and vexation in the world, observing that a little pleasure was mingled with numerous pains.[15] The girls should strive not to dishonor their illustrious ancestors by doing anything base or foolish. Night and day they were to address prayers and sighs to the invisible and intangible god. They were not to remain in bed through laziness but were to begin early to learn the work of spinning, weaving, grinding corn, or preparing food. In a warning against dishonoring parents one lord said:

Do not cast infamy over them by addicting yourself to carnal delights; do not throw yourself onto the filth and stench of lewdness. If you should reach that point it would be better for you to die at once.[16]

The girls were advised to accept the man who asked for them in marriage whether he was handsome or not.[17] They should live

[12] Sahagun, *Historie Génerále des Choses de la Nouvelle-Espagne*, pp. 382-83.
[13] *Ibid.*, pp. 383-84.
[14] *Ibid.*, pp. 397-98.
[15] *Ibid.*, p. 385.
[16] *Ibid.*, p. 388.
[17] *Ibid.*, p. 389.

faithfully with their husbands and not leave them, "provided they were not poor laborers, mechanics, or ordinary men of low origin." [18]

Grandmothers urged girls to preserve their chastity in youth and to be faithful to their husbands. They were reminded that, if they were caught in adultery, the law of the world was that they should be "punished by death, thrown into the street, where their heads would be crushed, and their bodies dragged on the ground." [19]

A discourse of the king to the people showed that the children were not the only ones who received instruction. The king seemed to be especially anxious to combat drunkenness:

> From drunkenness proceed adultery, rape, seduction of virgins, and violence against relatives and allies; from it come theft, brigandage, and attacks with armed hand; from it still proceed curses, false witnesses, slanders, separations, quarrels and wranglings. . . . All this is the fruit of the octli and of drunkenness. [20]

This tendency to instruct the old as well as the young was by no means limited to the Aztecs. Similar practices will be seen in some of the other educational methods studied.

THE EDUCATION OF THE PUEBLO CHILD

The territory occupied by the Pueblos extended through northern New Mexico and Arizona. [21] The region is elevated and semi-arid but the soil produces well when irrigated. As wild game could not be found in abundance, the population had to depend upon agriculture as the main source of food. Thus the climate and the soil were important factors in developing permanent locations for the small groups and in lessening the occasions for conflicts with others.

As a result of such conditions the Pueblo villages were occupied by a sedentary population devoted very largely to the arts of peace. Although several linguistic stocks [22] were represented, only minor cultural differences are found, demonstrating the influence of the geography on life and thought. [23]

[18] *Ibid.*, p. 366.
[19] *Ibid.*, p. 393.
[20] *Ibid.*, p. 366.
[21] Spencer, *Education of the Pueblo Child*, p. 10. Goddard, *Indians of the Southwest*, pp. 15, 67-68.
[22] Goddard, *Indians of the Southwest*, pp. 67-68.
[23] Spencer, *op. cit.*, pp. 16-17.

For defense against nomadic tribes these Indians lived in well-built communal houses of stone or adobe.[24] Their government was largely under religious control, the main officers being appointed by the priesthood. Many of their religious ceremonies followed the form of dramas in which masked actors represented their gods.[25] These actors were no doubt important factors in fixing religious ideas in the minds of children.

Both Mrs. Stevenson and Spencer emphasize the fact that parents were very affectionate toward their children. On the other hand, children were respectful and obedient. Spencer says:

> The implicit obedience of children, their marked respect for their elders, the kindness of parents to children, their natural helpfulness, generous hospitality, forbearance, and industry are all marked characteristics of these people.
>
> In the wildest, roughest plays of the children or in the most intensely exciting games of adults, no Pueblo will angrily strike another. It would be beneath his dignity. The child who would disdain the counsel of his parents or refuse to obey unquestionably their commands would be looked upon with horror; yet no harsh means are used in attaining this result. For him a better way has been found.
>
> The Pueblo child does not receive commands to do or refrain from doing without the reason for the command being given. This reason is given in the form of a story in which the given action is portrayed with the good or evil resulting to the doer.[26]

The last paragraph quoted is a little too broad in its statement. Nevertheless, the effectiveness of these stories was assured through the influence of superstitious fear which was no doubt strengthened by the fact that the grandfathers of the village were "the story-tellers, the primitive schoolmasters and historians of the tribe." [27] Stories told by such men in a solemn half-chant, when the evening light of the room was dim, could not but have a profound emotional effect.

Pueblo religious ceremonies added to the power of superstition in the control of conduct. At the age of four or five, boys, and sometimes girls, were initiated into their secret organizations. Mrs. Stevenson has described the ceremony as it was performed among the Zuñi. The initiation into the order of the Kok-ko came every four years. Actors with masks impersonated the

[24] Goddard, *op. cit.*, pp. 70-71.

[25] *Ibid.*, p. 100.

[26] Spencer, *op cit.*, pp. 79-81.

[27] *Ibid.*, p. 80.

Kok-ko, their ancestral gods. The child, however, was led to believe that the actors were the gods themselves. In their kivas, or places for religious ceremonies, various symbolic rites were performed before the child. Each boy was accompanied by a godfather. As one feature, the boy was held on the back of the godfather who stretched a blanket around him while he was beaten with bunches of Spanish bayonet in the hands of the Kok-ko.[28] On another occasion the boy grasped the knee of his godfather and was beaten in a similar manner.

During one of the rites the child drew in the breath which the Kok-ko blew onto a wand. This was considered necessary before any child could enter the kiva of the Kok-ko after death.[29] While the ceremonies were going on, the godfather offered prayers and gave the boy instruction. The ceremonies continued several nights, and during four days the boy abstained from animal food.[30]

After several years the boy voluntarily decided whether he would assume the vow that had been taken for him by his godfather. If he desired to be initiated, he was again beaten by the Kok-ko who, at this time, removed their masks and told the youth that they had been instructed by the gods to represent them.

Pueblo parents taught their children "obedience, industry, modesty, and especially the avoidance of evil sorcery of all kinds," [31] relying almost entirely on the fear of the supernatural. One can readily see how their teachings were reinforced by the religious ceremonies performed in the village.

Good advice was not reserved for children alone. When a young man was about to marry, the girl's father gave him the following counsel:

> You are about to marry my daughter. You must work hard; you must watch the sheep and help to cut the wood and plant grain and cut it.

The girl's mother reminded him to be kind to his wife.[32]

PIMA EDUCATION

The home of the Pima Indians was in southwestern Arizona. On the southern trail to California many of the pioneers owed

[28] Stevenson, *The Religious Life of the Zuñi Child*, p. 551.
[29] *Ibid.*, p. 548.
[30] *Ibid.*, p. 553.
[31] Spencer, *op. cit.*, p. 81.
[32] Stevenson, *The Zuñi Indians*, p. 304.

their lives to the friendly attitude of these native farmers of
the Southwest. They were very valuable to the whites in the
contest with the Apache. Their valleys were covered with ruins
of prehistoric buildings and the remains of a high degree of civilization. They were tillers of irrigated land, and vegetable food
predominated in their diet. However, about once in five years
the Gila River failed. This drove the Pima to seek "animal
food, roots, berries, and especially the edible agave" in the Apache
country.[33] Thus we find a basis for their military instruction to
the boy. Yet, living in an area of intensive agriculture, they
showed an appreciation of the virtues of peace.

When still quite young, the Pima boy was taken up by his
father at daybreak and told "something of the mysteries of the
great Sun god." [34] As he grew older his father required him
to listen to his lectures on the behavior of the warrior and the
citizen. Inattention caused the father's stiffened middle finger
to strike the boy's nose and bring his head to the proper attitude.

He was trained to go on scout duty or to look after the live
stock before his morning meal. He was always told to be alert
and skillful with his bow and arrows, ready to repulse the Apache.
By the following words he was taught by his father to become accustomed to cold and hunger in order to endure the long march
into the Apache country:

If you are wounded in battle, don't make a great outcry about it like a
child. Pull out the arrow and slip away; or, if hard stricken, die with
a silent throat. Go on the war trail with a small blanket. It is light and
protection enough for one aided by the magicians. Inure yourself to the
cold while yet a boy. Fight not at all with your comrades, preserve your
strength for the combat with the Apaches. Then, if brave, will come to
you high honor. Be unselfish or you will not be welcome at the fire of
the friendly. The selfish man is lonely, and his untended fire dies. Keep
your peace when a foolish man addresses the people. Join not in his
imprudent councilings. Above all, talk not foolishly yourself. Bathe in
the cold water of the early morning, that you may be prepared for the
purification ceremony after killing an enemy.[35]

The boy also learned that if he conformed to the advice given
him he would be more desirable as a husband. At about the
age of twenty the youth spent four days and nights with the
keeper of the legends.

[33] Russell, *The Pima Indians*, p. 66.
[34] *Ibid.*, p. 190.
[35] *Ibid.*, p. 190.

The mother was supposed to give her daughter proper instruction. However, if she were careless or indifferent, the father assumed the task himself. Indifference on the part of both parents was rare. Russell gives the following speech of a father to his daughter:

> Stay at home with your mother. Watch and help her handle the cooking pots, the mortar, and metate, that you may know how to prepare the seeds of Pimeria. Keep the fire alive and have wood ever ready. See that the drinking olla is never empty. If you do these things well, you will not gad about after you are married and leave your hearth vacant so that your husband may come home to find the fire out or to put it out to your discomfiture; for it is the office of man to kindle the fire but the part of woman to keep it burning.[36]

At seven or eight, girls began to help in the cooking, and at the age of nine or ten they began to make baskets, at which task some showed their laziness. They made rag dolls and played family activities with them, including funerals. Their little dishes were molded from mud.

In the evenings they played "puberty dances" and listened to the wonderful tales of prowess of their elders or the adventures of the mythical animals of ancient Pimeria.

At the age of eleven or twelve, the puberty dance was celebrated for girls. For four days the girl was in charge of a preceptress, a favorite woman, not a relative, who gave her instruction concerning household tasks and the "principles of industry, honesty, chastity, and the like." Certain taboos were enforced. She was taught that to scratch her head with her finger would cause lice, and that her teeth would fall out if she blew the fire. The two remained apart from their families during this period. If her parents could afford to provide the feast, friends were invited to the dance which required the whole of four nights. The best girls were selected to dance with one who was "coming out."

The Pima boy was taught industry, forbearance, unselfishness, courage, and fortitude, while the girl was taught application to household tasks, industry, honesty, and chastity.

The Education of the Boy among the Santee Sioux

The characteristics of the Plains Indians will be given in some detail in Chapter IV. It is sufficient to say here merely that these

[36] *Ibid.*, p. 191

Indians depended largely on wild game for food and were almost constantly engaged in war.

Eastman's *Indian Boyhood* pictures life among the Santee Sioux of the Dakota [37] around 1870. Although Eastman was born at Redwood Falls, Minnesota, his band moved several times on account of wars. His mother died in his infancy, and when he was five years old, his father was captured by the whites. He was reared by his father's mother and her son, his uncle. His story of his life up to the age of fifteen gives us a good idea of the education of children in the family and in the village.

To begin with, Eastman, the youngest of five boys, was called Hakadah, "the pitiful last," a name which he had to carry until he could win another.[38] In his early years his grandmother would sing to him a lullaby which, he says, ran like this:

> Sleep, sleep, my boy, the Chippewas
>   Are far away—are far away.
> Sleep, sleep, my boy, prepare to meet
>   The foe by day—the foe by day!
> The cowards will not dare to fight
>   Till morning break—till morning break.
> Sleep, sleep, my child, while still 'tis night;
>   Then bravely wake—then bravely wake.[39]

The ideal of the warrior was thus presented even before the child could understand his language.

As soon as children left the cradle their attention was directed to objects of their environment. "The robin was calling his mate to share his food. The thrush was singing for his wife. The whippoorwill might be an Ojibway scout." [40] At night the child was told that the owl was watching outside. A legend of a crying child stolen by the owl kept children quiet in the darkness.[41] As he grew older, Hakadah's uncle, in the early morning, told him to look closely at what he saw during the day. In the evening the boy was questioned concerning his observations. If his answers showed a superficial view, he was told to take a second look as the wolf did while running away.[42] He was instructed to learn about the different wild animals by studying them unobserved.

---

[37] For characteristics of the Plains Indians, see Chapter IV.
[38] Eastman, *Indian Boyhood*, p. 4.
[39] *Ibid.*, p. 7.
[40] *Ibid.*, p. 9.
[41] *Ibid.*, p. 10.
[42] *Ibid.*, pp. 52, 54.

Boys were expected to endure hardship as a preparation for the life of the warrior and the hunter. The man was expected to be able to go without food for three days and to run for a day and a night.[43] In order to train Hakadah to go without food his uncle would challenge him to fast during the day. Boys, who were being trained in this way, would blacken their faces to show what they were doing. Hakadah's playmates would help develop his self-control by offering him their choicest morsels before sunset.[44] His uncle would sometimes give a loud yell or fire a gun early in the morning so that he might become accustomed to surprises.[45] In camp in a strange place, his uncle would, after dark, send him repeatedly for water to try him out.[46]

In the evening, in the tipi, stories were recounted, which the children rehearsed. Their grandmother told them, "Be strong of heart; be patient!" She supplemented her advice with a story of how a young chief was killed by his own band for murdering a woman while in a rage.[47] The boys were taught to respect their elders and not to speak before them unless requested to do so.

Their grandmother would ask the children: "What bird shows most judgment in caring for its young?" One child favored the eagle and another the oriole. Reasons were called for. The eagle's lofty nest was safe from all harm. High in the air, its young became accustomed to hunger and hardships; the cold and the storm therefore made them like the warrior. The oriole suspended its nest in such a way that no enemy could reach it, thus providing a safe and a more comfortable home.[48]

The boys were allowed the greatest freedom to hunt or play as they wished. In regard to their sports Eastman comments as follows:

Our sports were molded by the life and customs of our people; indeed, we practiced only what we expected to do when grown. Our games were feats with the bow and arrow, foot and pony races, wrestling, swimming, and imitation of the customs and habits of our fathers. We had sham fights with mud balls and willow wands; we played lacrosse, made war upon bees, shot winter arrows (which were used only in that season), coasted upon the ribs of animals and buffalo robes.[49]

[43] *Ibid.*, p. 56.
[44] *Ibid.*, p. 57.
[45] *Ibid.*
[46] *Ibid.*, p. 58.
[47] *Ibid.*, pp. 51, 59.
[48] *Ibid.*, pp. 79-81.
[49] *Ibid.*, p. 64.

Some of these contests were severe and dangerous but they were similar to the activities of the men, so the boys engaged in them with intense interest.

Children were taught that all the customs of their people were instituted by the supernatural powers.[50]   In addition to hearing stories in the family tipi, children visited old men who told the legends of the tribes thus reïnforcing the attitude of the family.[51] From the time Hakadah was five years old, when his father was captured, all the boys were constantly reminded of their duty to avenge his supposed death.

As a reward for his contribution toward a lacrosse victory for his side, Hakadah's name was changed to Ohiyesa, "the winner." [52]

When children grew older, chastity was brought to their attention.   A maidens' feast was provided in which only chaste maidens could participate.   By touching a stone and some arrows, each maiden declared her purity.   Any young man could question a girl's statement, but a false challenge might almost cost him his life.[53]   The boys had a similar feast for those who had never spoken to a girl in the way of courtship.   It was considered ridiculous to do so before attaining some honor as a warrior, and the novices prided themselves greatly upon their self-control in sex relations.[54]

THE BUFFALO CEREMONY

The Oglala of the Teton Dakota celebrated what was called the Buffalo Ceremony for a young woman at the age of puberty. While the rites were sometimes quite elaborate, the ceremony is presented here in connection with family education because the father, or the young woman's nearest kinsman, had to make preparation for certain ceremonial rites.   This man could also serve as conductor if he had qualified for the position.   Otherwise he had to secure a shaman for this purpose.   In any case, both parents participated prominently in the performance.

Believing that the influences of a young woman's life would be determined by the preponderance of good or evil during this period, they endeavored through the ceremony to obtain for her the guardianship of the Buffalo God, the patron of chastity,

50 Eastman, *Indian Boyhood*, p. 49.
51 *Ibid.*, pp. 115-37.
52 *Ibid.*, p. 45.
53 *Ibid.*, pp. 181-87.
54 *Ibid.*, p. 183.

fecundity, industry, and hospitality. A certain standing in social affairs was secured for one who had been honored with the rites.[55]

On the day preceding the ceremony, families began to arrive in response to invitations to attend. Social festivities incident to the gathering lasted well into the night while the young woman remained alone for meditation in a new tipi.

As dawn of the next day approached, the shaman, with his face toward the east, sang:

> A voice, anpeo, hear it.
> Speak low, hear it.[56]

Anpeo meant the red aurora, who should be invoked in this way for a pleasant day. As in other religious rites, the Indians began their celebration with a reverent appeal to the powers.

Various songs and rites followed for the purpose of keeping off Iktomi who could make women foolish, Anog Ite, the deceitful woman who incited women to do shameful things, Wazi, the wizard who might nullify their undertakings, and Hohnogica, who might cause the woman trouble when she was a mother.[57]

At the beginning of one of these rites, the young woman sat with her legs crossed as did the men and the children. At the close, she was told that she should now be ashamed to sit in this way, and her mother arranged her feet together as the women held theirs. After this to sit with her legs crossed would indicate that she was a lewd woman.

For what followed, Walker's own version of the speech of the conductor of the ceremony is worth quoting:

I sought a vision and saw the messenger of the white buffalo cow. I sang this song:

> The messenger of the buffalo in the west.
> The messenger of the buffalo in the west.
> I will give you a robe.

Then the messenger said: "A spider; a turtle; the voice of a lark; a brave man; children; a tipi smoking." I have spoken with the Gods and I will tell you what these things mean. The spider is an industrious woman. She builds a tipi for her children. She gives them plenty of food. The turtle is a wise woman. She hears many things and says nothing. Her skin is a shield. An arrow cannot wound her. The lark is a cheerful

[55] Walker, *The Sun Dance and Other Ceremonies of the Oglala Division of the Teton Dakota*, p. 141.

[56] *Ibid.*, p. 142.

[57] *Ibid.*, pp. 145-46.

woman. She brings pleasant weather. She does not scold. She is always happy. If a brave man takes you for his woman you may sing his scalp song and you may dance his scalp dance. He will kill plenty of game. You will have plenty of meat and skins. You will bear him many children and you will be happy. There will always be a fire in your tipi, and you will have food for your people. If you are industrious like the spider; if you are wise like the turtle; if you are cheerful like the lark, then you will be chosen by a brave man, and you will have plenty and never be ashamed. These things I saw in the vision: A coyote; worn moccasins; and I heard a voice in mourning. The Buffalo God sends this message to you. If you listen to Iktomi, or to Iya, or to Anog Ite, then you will be lazy and lewd and poor and miserable. A brave man or a good hunter will not give a dog for you. Your robe will be old and ragged. Your moccasins will be worn and without color on them. The buffalo horns are on my head, and I speak for the Buffalo God. The buffalo tail is behind me, and this makes my word sacred. I am now the buffalo bull, and you are a young buffalo cow. I will show you what the bad influences would have you do. I will show you what the good influences would have you do.[58]

After a ceremonial smoke and a song, the conductor, to the sound of the drum and rattles, danced from the door of the lodge to one side of the young woman, then to the door and to the other side, back and forth several times with increasing vigor until, at last, his step became frantic. Then on the outside, "on his hands and knees, he bellowed and pawed the ground as a bull does, and sniffed the air as if trying to locate something by scent. Entering the lodge on his hands and knees, he sidled against the young woman, first on one side and then on the other. Each time he came the mother placed some sage under the arm and in the lap of her daughter." After this the conductor addressed the young woman:

That is the manner in which the Crazy Buffalo will approach you to tempt you to do things that will make you ashamed and will make your people ashamed of you. Your mother showed you in what manner you can drive away the evil things that would harm you. She will teach you how to do this. If you remember this a man will pay the price for you, and you will be proud of your children.[59]

If a man paid the price of six buffalo robes for a woman, it brought her an honorable distinction of which the women were quite proud.[60]

[58] Walker, *The Sun Dance and Other Ceremonials of the Oglaga Division of the Teton Dakota*, p. 147.
[59] *Ibid.*, p. 148.
[60] *Ibid.*

The conductor then, while singing, mixed chokeberries with water in a wooden bowl and in these words told the young woman to drink from it as the buffalo did at the water hole:

The water in it is red and made so by the Buffalo God, and it is for buffalo women. Drink from it.

Afterwards the conductor drank from it in the same manner and passed it around requesting all the friends of the young woman to partake.

After the young woman had made a ceremonial gift of a dress to the buffalo woman, the conductor gave her some sage to eat, saying, "Sage is bitter, but your mother has shown you how to use it." Then he gave her sweetgrass to chew, saying it pleased the gods and that she should remember these things. Two wands of Buffalo charms were presented her, in order to keep away the two-faced woman, Anog Ite, and to bring many children. Under the conductor's direction the mother then arranged the young woman's hair in two strands so that they hung in front after the fashion of the women and not behind as the girls wore theirs.[61]

CHASTITY AMONG THE HUPA

In many tribes a man showed his appreciation of his bride by paying her family liberally. Among the Hupa, according to Dr. Goddard, it was not only considered an honor for the woman if the man had given a good price for her but it also presumed a high standard of conduct for her and for her children. "If a man behaved improperly, people would say: 'What is the matter? His mother was well paid for.'"

Girls were often directed to observe the conduct of careless people. They were told that nobody would pay much for them if they were not chaste. No illegitimate person was allowed to enter the Indians' sacred house or their sweathouse where ceremonies were held. One of Dr. Goddard's informants told how a man trailed his faithless wife and a man to the woods and killed them both. Women took their daughters out to see the dead bodies to impress upon them the consequences of such action.

The author is also indebted to Dr. Goddard for information concerning the method of giving the individual necessary knowledge upon the subject of exogamy. In answer to Dr. Goddard's inquiries upon the subject, his interpreter said that when, as a

[61] *Ibid.*, p. 149.

boy, he attended ceremonies and gatherings his mother was constantly calling his attention to certain girls or women who were his relatives and whom he, consequently, should not think of marrying.

The Arapaho Father to his Son

Kroeber gives a hypothetical speech of the father of a young man at his marriage to a Cheyenne woman. After expressing his appreciation of the kindness shown him by the Cheyenne, the father proceeded to address his son:

My son, it pleases me much where you found a woman. My son, disregard it, even if there is something unpleasant for you to hear. Even if your own wife strikes you, disregard it, and even if the others say what you do not like to listen to. Where you are a servant, you must not mind it. Try hard, my son, not to become discouraged too quickly. Do not be bashful, but be kind. Do good where you are united. Whatever your father-in-law orders you to do, my son, or your mother-in-law, or your brother-in-law, do that for them. Do not go away without the consent of your wife. Do not roam about without purpose, my son, but do your best where you offered yourself as servant. In the former life of the people it was good to be a servant. If I might be young, I should be providing food for all; but what we lived on is gone. Do your best in planting, which we are shown by the whites, my son. Do whatever you are told, and water your animals carefully. Love your wife's parents, and love her people. Be pleasant to persons who come to your tent, my son. When friends come where you are serving, they will be Cheyenne who come. When the Cheyenne arrive, say to them, "Well, come in." Do not be bashful, for you are now united to them. Do not scold your wife. Always treat her well and pity her. Those who try to be good are treated well and pitied. Do your best, and do not become tired. And now look at your tent, your pipe, your food, and your friends.[62]

In his counsel the father clearly showed the position of the husband in his wife's family and his own ideal of forbearance and affection in the husband's attitude toward his wife.

Advice of a Pawnee Mother

In his *Pawnee Hero Stories and Folk Tales*, Grinnell records the advice given Lone Chief, a historical character, by his mother. The widow of a chief, she had supported the boy by raising corn, beans, and pumpkins. She taught him how he should act, urged him to be a man, and to remember how she had worked for him. She said:

[62] Kroeber, *The Arapaho*, pp. 315-16.

You must always trust in Tirawa. He made us, and through him we live. When you grow up, you must be a man. Be brave and face whatever danger may meet you. . . . When you get to be a man, remember that it is ambition that makes the man. If you go on the warpath, do not turn around when you have gone part way, but go on as far as you were going and then come back. . . . I want you to think about the hard times we have been through. Take pity on the people who are poor, because we have been poor, and people have taken pity on us. If I live to see you a man, and to go off on the warpath, I would not cry if I were to hear that you had been killed in battle. That is what makes a man: to fight and to be brave. . . . Love your friend, never desert him. If you see him surrounded by the enemy, do not run away. Go to him, be killed together, and let your bones lie side by side.

According to Pawnee tradition Lone Chief was a worthy son and was made a chief on account of his character and exploits.[63]

The Crow Chief's Address to Young Men

Curtis states that a Crow chief would sometimes call the young men into his lodge to address them as follows:

Young men, look at me, see my face. All men have flesh; all men have hearts; all men know what death is. About you are enemies surrounding your whole country. If you have a gun, remember it; if you have bow and arrows, remember that. The moment comes when the enemy charges upon you, stand firm, and remember your hearts—keep them brave. . . . The people who surround us are foolish; they have no pity; they do not care for the old. But you, when you chase the Buffalo, remember the poor; share your meat with them. . . . When you marry, she is your wife. If you have sickness, she will stay many nights by you while your brother sleeps. Do not strike her; be kind to her. Only the wise will hear my words; the foolish will hear them now, but when I pass they will forget.[64]

The Crow were constantly at war with all their neighbors. Hence the chief stated the facts when he said that they were surrounded by enemies. The warrior should be brave in facing the enemy and kind to his family and his people.

The Fast

Among many tribes, the youth at the age of twelve or fifteen retired from the village to fast alone in order that he might obtain a vision of some object or animal which afterwards was considered his guardian spirit.[65] The Ojibway and the Menomini parents had someone keep watch so that the boy should not

[63] Grinnell, *Pawnee Hero Stories and Folk Tales*, pp. 45-47.
[64] Curtis, *The North American Indian*, Vol. IV, pp. 19-21.
[65] Wissler, *The American Indian*, pp. 197.

become entirely exhausted.[66] Eastman's statement already given shows how the boys were trained to fast at home. Dunbar said that he had observed Pawnee travel three days without food "and utter no complaint, nor remit perceptibly anything of their wonted activity." [67] Training in the ability to go without food was no doubt begun fairly early in the life of the boy.

Moral Teachings in Family and Village Life

One of the first observations to be made from the study of family education in several different tribes or nations is that provisions for the instruction and training of youth were not uniform. Furthermore, the principles that have been advanced as a basis for classification are difficult to apply. Todd, referring to Herbert Spencer's statement that warlike peoples are strict in training their children and that peaceable peoples are more lax, concludes that the statement offers little help.[68] Not only does it offer little help but the opposite seems to be true in North America. In Mexico and among the Pueblos we find obedience to parents to be one of the first qualities taught. In Mexico governesses and pages accompanied the children of the nobility, for the specific purpose of curtailing their liberty of speech and of action. On the other hand, Eastman informs us that boys of the Santee Sioux were allowed the greatest freedom. Miss Paget in *The People of the Plains* says:

> The youngsters were actually adored, and consequently would impress a stranger as being very badly brought up. They were never corrected for any faults but, up to a certain age, did as they pleased, when, of their own accord, they seemed to realize the respect due to their parents. This was in a measure about the way the older Indians treated the younger ones. No disrespect to elders was tolerated, and when the children were supposed to have reached years of discretion they were soon made to understand this, not by their parents, but by their relatives and friends.[69]

Observations made by Grinnell and Dunbar indicate that Eastman and Miss Paget have stated the practices generally followed by the warlike tribes.

It can be said that education among the warlike tribes appealed

[66] Hoffman, *Midewiwin or Grand Medicine Society of the Ojibwa*, p. 163. *The Menomini Indians*, p. 164.
[67] Dunbar, *The Pawnee Indians; Their History and Ethnology, Magazine of American History*, 1880, p. 263.
[68] Todd, *The Primitive Family as an Educational Agency*, p. 148.
[69] Paget, *The People of the Plains*, p. 119.

more to the instinctive tendencies of the individual, while among sedentary peoples education had to depend more on ideas that had been acquired. Warlike tribes were inclined to provide for moral training which was supplemented by instruction. The sedentary groups tended more to impart instruction in abstract statements of their ideals.

In all the areas studied, even in family education, children were given reasons for most of the virtues taught. In Mexico the reasons were expressed largely in abstract form. Among the Pueblos the virtues were given a setting in a myth which utilized superstition to secure compliance. On the Plains the habits of birds and animals often served as a starting point for teaching. The good of the individual appears to have been the prevailing motive in education. The individual's own welfare was more clearly conceived than any other aim.

General social approval and disapproval were the most potent factors in the development of the desired attitudes and behavior on the part of children. Miss Paget states how the Plains Indians made use of this method. If a boy above a certain age did not conduct himself properly he was admonished once or twice by relatives or friends. She says:

If this advice was ignored, he was ignored also; and the rest of the band followed suit, so that the youth soon found that the best policy was not to look upon himself any longer as a spoilt child.[70]

In this way public opinion and ridicule, to which the Indians were extremely sensitive,[71] reïnforced the teachings of the family.

The aims of family education were determined by the activities of the adult. Many of these activities were simply imitated blindly by the children. Various customs and taboos were perpetuated through a blind superstitious fear of the unseen powers. On the other hand, ideas of ethical morality were frequently developed by sound reasoning based on human experience.

While various factors were involved in the development of character, the family was the first agency in primitive life to become clearly conscious of its educational function. It undertook specifically to transmit to children the ideals of the tribe and to develop conformity to the manners and usages generally approved. Furthermore, society recognized this obligation of the

[70] *Ibid.*, p. 120.
[71] *Ibid.*, p. 123.

family and, through public opinion, held the family responsible for its fulfillment. Among the Hupa, in certain cases, if a man behaved improperly a question was raised concerning the character of his mother. Among the Aztecs shameful conduct was a disgrace to the parents. In the Oglala sun dance, on the occasion of the piercing of children's ears, parents obligated themselves to rear their child so that he would conform to the laws and customs of the Oglala.[72]

[72] Walker, *op. cit.*, p. 119.

CHAPTER IV

THE IDEALS PRESENTED IN THE SUN DANCE AND IN MILITARY SOCIETIES

The main source of food and clothing for the Indians of the Plains was the buffalo. Their hunts carried them away from their more permanent villages and into conflict with the interests of other tribes with the same needs. Without the protection of insurmountable natural barriers they were open to attack by hostile neighbors. In the sixteenth century horses were introduced. On account of the service that they rendered they soon became the basis for estimating the wealth of their owners. By reason of the facility with which they could be transported, they became very tempting movable property. The horse could not only carry himself but he could add speed to the flight of his captor. Among peoples without a standard of morality that went very far beyond their own kith and kin, it is easy to see how such conditions could develop a type of hostile undertaking in the form of small marauding parties organized for the purpose of capturing horses from neighboring tribes.

Much of the warfare of the Indians of the Plains was carried on in this way or originated in such enterprises. A man would invite several friends into his tipi and inform them of his intention of going on the warpath. Frequently some of them would decline because they had promised to join some other party or did not wish to go at that time. Later, others often heard of the proposal and asked permission to enlist. Soon a band of from six to fifteen men was ready to go out to seek adventure—and horses. The organizer was the recognized leader to whom each member of the party owed implicit obedience. Those who did not have confidence in him refused to join.

When such a party approached a hostile village, they did not make an open attack but concealed themselves until nightfall when, under cover of the darkness, they crept stealthily into the camp, located desirable horses, cut the ropes by which they were tied, and rode them out to their rendezvous where they took an inventory and decided whether to search for more horses or to start immediately for home. If they did not meet any member

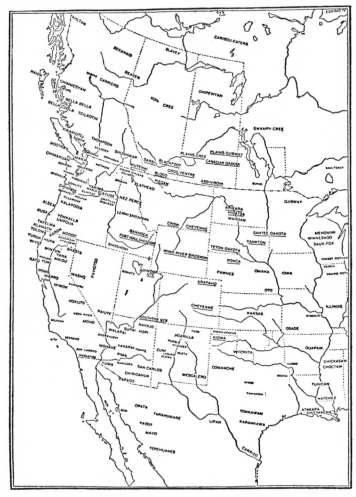

DISTRIBUTION OF TRIBES HAVING THE SUN DANCE
The tribes underlined are those that have the Sun Dance ceremony.
From Spier, *The Sun Dance of the Plains Indians: Its Development and Diffusion.*

of the hostile group, there was frequently no bloodshed as a result of the undertaking. Typical orations of warriors in the Plains-Cree sun dance give the following details:

We were camped at such and such a place. From there a war party went out. I was one. We numbered so many. So many nights we walked, hiding in the daytime. Suddenly we felt the enemy. We sent out scouts. They found a large camp. Three days we stayed there; we saw them every day, but they never felt us. We brought away twenty horses. I cut loose one tied to the door of a lodge. Three days we fled. They never overtook us.

A tap or two on the drum at each sentence and a loud and long rattle at the end show the appreciation of the audience. Or the speech may run thus:

We started out from the Elbow on a hunting tour. We came across people on the edge of the Eagle Hills. We were a large camp. We struck out on the prairie. On the tenth night the Blackfoot attacked us. We beat them off. For three days we fought as we traveled. I was riding a buffalo runner, a bay with three white feet. I exchanged shots with a Blackfoot. I rode at him. He ran away. I caught him and pulled him off his horse. I stabbed him with a knife.[1]

If the marauders encountered members of the other tribe or if the raid were discovered in time, a large number of the enemy would dash forth to chase the intruders and would sometimes annihilate them. This action would call for reprisals by which hunting parties or unprotected camps of old men, women, and children were sometimes exterminated. Such petty warfare kept warriors always ready to fight.

In a sense, war to the Indians of the Plains was a great game in which their interest was in every way commensurate with the great odds at stake—the life or death of the players. Nevertheless, certain rules were frequently observed between warring tribes so that some battles resulted in as few fatalities as were counted at many of our football games twenty-five years ago. Grinnell describes how these battles took place as late as the decade 1860 to 1870:

About sunrise the Sioux would ride up over the hills in a line fronting toward the village. They appeared mounted on their best ponies, clad in their most elaborate war costume, and wearing long war bonnets of the feathers of the war eagle, which almost swept the ground as their horses curveted along to the music of the monotonous but thrilling war chant. At the instant of their appearance the Pawnee village would begin to stir like a disturbed ant hill. The shouts of command by the men, the piercing calls from women, the alarmed and excited shrieks of the children, the neighing and heavy hoofbeats of the horses, the barking and howling of the dogs, as they were kicked out of the way, made a very Babel of sounds.[2]

[1] Robert Jefferson, in Goddard's *Notes on the Sun Dance of the Plains-Cree in Alberta*, p. 309.

[2] Grinnell, *Pawnee Hero Stories and Folk-Tales*, p. 313.

Snatching their weapons, the men rode out to meet the enemy. The Sioux remained in line awaiting the Pawnee who advanced chanting their war songs and yelling defiance. The lines halted six or seven hundred yards apart. From one side a warrior would then ride out in front of the line and address his party, belittling the enemy and praising his comrades. He closed with an account of his own brave deeds and then, bending low on his horse, he dashed toward one end of the hostile line. Within bowshot he rode along the front, shooting arrow after arrow. Those whom he had passed rushed in pursuit until the whole party was riding headlong after the defiant warrior. If the latter received no injury, he was not followed very far on his return to his own men. If he was wounded or overtaken, his tribesmen charged to rescue him, and hand-to-hand fighting ensued. Men were bruised and gashed, and occasionally a man was killed in the mêlée. If the warrior who had led out was killed and scalped, his party withdrew at once, both sides taking their former positions. Then a man from the other side would ride out as the first warrior had done, and the fight would open again.

Sometimes a daring or desperate warrior would charge through the enemy's line and shoot some particular man, count coup on him, and scalp him. The enemy would try to kill him, his friends would rush to his aid, and another fierce struggle would then take place. Similar fighting would continue sometimes through the day, with a loss of only one or two men on either side, until one party "would become discouraged and would break and run." [3]

With such an experience it is not at all surprising that warfare should affect practically all of the thinking of the Indians of the Plains. In his account of Crow military societies Lowie, after asserting that they had many nonmilitary features, says:

Nevertheless, we must remember, as does Professor Kroeber in discussing a corresponding Arapaho feature, that war loomed so large in the consciousness of the Plains Indian that it could not help coloring his every activity. [4]

However, we should not conclude from this view that the Indian was anxious to sacrifice himself for his people. He engaged in warfare on account of his instinct for it and his desire for booty and glory. His reluctance to accept a military position that meant certain death will be shown in the study of the Crow soci-

[3] Grinnell, *Pawnee Hero Stories and Folk Tales*, p. 316.
[4] Lowie, *Military Societies of the Crow Indians*, p. 150.

eties. Long life was also desired. Spier says that any Kiowa could enter the sun dance with the object of becoming a better warrior and living a long time.[5] Possibly the best expression of this is found in a Kiowa warrior's prayer:

May this medicine render me brave in war, proof against the weapons of my enemies, strong in the chase, wise in council; and finally, may it preserve me to a good old age, and may I at last die in peace among my own people.[6]

A detailed discussion of the available information on the particular culture of each tribe presented in this chapter would throw some light on our main subject but would not add greatly to the significance of the results. The Siouan language was represented on the Plains by the Assiniboin, Crow, Dakota, Hidasta, Iowa, Kansa, Mandan, Missouri, Omaha, Osage, Oto, and Ponca. The Algonkian tongue was represented by the Arapaho, Blackfoot, Cheyenne, Gros Ventre, Plains-Cree, and Plains Ojibway. The Caddoan linguistic family included the Arikara, Pawnee, and Wichita on the Plains. Other language stocks were the Kiowan, the Shoshonean, the Athapascan, and the Shahaptian.[7] Wissler says that there is little correspondence between the linguistic stocks and the culture type,[8] thus emphasizing the importance of the culture area in determining the habits and customs of the Indian.

In the sun dance and in military societies, we find how warlike ideals were worked into the ceremonies and social organizations of the Plains.

The Sun Dance

The sun dance was the most widespread ceremony performed by the Indians of the Plains. In its complex organization were included numerous rites frequently found in other rituals. From tribe to tribe some features retained in one ritual disappeared from another, and local influence was practically always found. In a comparative study of descriptions of the sun dance in nineteen different tribes, Spier gives a table of eighty-two particular features of which no tribe performed more than fifty-four.[9] In

[5] Spier, *Notes on the Kiowa Sun Dance*, p. 445.
[6] *Ibid.*, p. 449.
[7] Wissler, *North American Indians of the Plains*, p. 135.
[8] *Ibid.*, p. 12.
[9] Spier, *The Sun Dance of the Plains Indians: Its Development and Diffusion*, pp. 464-66, 478.

tracing the origin of the sun dance, Spier, in his investigation, is inclined to give a slight priority to the Arapaho over the Cheyenne and to consider the Oglala as a third important center of diffusion.[10]

As our purpose is to describe only the incidental moral teachings, no detailed account of the sun dance will be undertaken. Spier has made an excellent summary from his comparative study:

The sun dance is usually initiated by some man or woman in fulfillment of a vow made at a time of distress, when supernatural aid is invoked and received. It is however not so much a thanks offering as a new occasion for supplicating supernatural power. On the formation of the camp circle, a tipi is pitched near its center in which the secret preliminary rites take place. Here the pledger and his associates are instructed in its esoteric significance by the priest conducting the ceremony, regalia are prepared, and painting and songs rehearsed. At the same time, more public preliminary activities are going forward. Some tribes prepare buffalo tongues for use during the dance, while special hunters are sent out to obtain a buffalo bull hide. Other parties are engaged in gathering timbers and brush for the dance structure, which they erect at the center of the camp circle. The spectacular performance begins when the great mass of people set out to fetch the center pole for the dance lodge: they scout for a tree, count coup on it, and fell it as if it were an enemy. The pledger and priests now leave the secret tipi for the dance lodge. A bundle of brush, the buffalo bull hide, cloth, and other offerings, are tied in the forks of the center pole; the pole is raised, and the structure soon completed.

Before the serious dancing commences, warriors dance in the lodge, and an altar is built there. The pledger and his associates, who deny themselves food and drink throughout this period, now begin to dance in supplication for supernatural power, steadily gazing the while at the sun or the offerings on the center pole. This lasts intermittently for several days and nights. Their sacrifice culminates in the so-called torture feature: skewers are thrust through the flesh of breast or back; by these they are tethered to the center pole, dancing and tearing against these bonds until the flesh gives away.[11]

The moral teachings appeared in the motives of the organizer or pledger, the prayers that were uttered, the moral requirements for the participants in different rites or activities, the recounting of warlike exploits, the discourses, and the example of endurance on the part of the dancer. It was a tribal ceremony, and practically the whole tribe witnessed its performance. Attendance was required of all except the sick and the feeble; this custom existed notably among the Cheyenne, the Oglala, and the Kiowa.[12]

[10] Spier, *The Sun Dance of the Plains Indians: Its Development and Diffusion*, pp. 494-95.

[11] *Ibid.*, pp. 461-62.

[12] *Ibid.*, p. 459.

The Crow police saw that all except "the very old men and women and the sick" were present and further notified them to keep still,[13] thereby giving a touch of our early colonial attitude toward church attendance and behavior.

The sun dance first of all taught coöperation. A master of ceremonies directed all the activities; and the whole tribe joined in the performance of the ceremony by participating in or witnessing its rites. Yet the purpose was always something sought by an individual or by individuals. Another important influence was the attitude toward the supernatural.[14] The sun dance showed the belief of the participants in the supernatural and their confidence in ceremonial procedure, in the fetish,[15] or in mortification of the flesh,[16] to secure the desired help from above.

Closely allied with these influences were the moral qualities implied in the purposes or vows of the organizers or pledgers. For instance, the Crow pledger, before going on the warpath, sought the vision of retaliation on the enemy who had killed a relative, magnifying the spirit of revenge.[17] The Blackfoot [18] and the Sarsi [19] undertook the sun dance to fulfill a vow made by a woman during the illness of a near relative. In this way the tribe honored the woman who felt her responsibility for her family.

Bravery, generosity, fortitude, and integrity,[20] the four great virtues of the Indian, were taught in various ways in the sun dance of the different tribes. The Oglala required that the candidate should possess these qualities and demanded general recognition by the people and special approval by the council as conditions for permission to undertake the ceremony. Generosity was to be shown in the provision of gifts and feasts for the participants.[21] Fortitude was demonstrated by the fast, the endurance of the torture, or the length of the dance itself. The Oglala considered willingness to endure pain for the accomplishment of a purpose

---

[13] Lowie, *The Sun Dance of the Crow Indians*, p. 30.

[14] Walker, *The Sun Dance and Other Ceremonies of the Oglala Division of the Teton Dakota*, p. 60.

[15] Wissler, *The Sun Dance of the Blackfoot Indians*, p. 229. Walker, *op. cit.*, p. 109.

[16] Lowie, *op. cit.*, p. 8. Walker, *op. cit.*, pp. 116-19.

[17] Lowie, *op. cit.*, pp. 7, 9.

[18] Wissler, *op. cit.*, p. 232.

[19] Goddard, *Notes on the Sun Dance of the Sarsi*, p. 275.

[20] Walker, *op. cit.*, p. 62.

[21] Walker, *op cit.*, pp. 62, 104. Goddard, *op. cit.*, p. 278; *Notes on the Sun Dance of the Cree in Alberta*, p. 310. Wissler, *op. cit.*, p. 249. Lowie, *op. cit.*, pp. 10, 33. *Sun Dance of the Ute*, p. 409.

the necessary guarantee of the sincerity and fortitude of the candidate.[22] This attitude was characteristic of the tribes that required the torture, though both ideas were not always present.[23] The common method of torture was to lift the skin and flesh on the breast or back of the dancer, cut a hole through and insert a skewer to which a thong could be attached. Sometimes this thong was tied to the lodge pole during the dance; some used four skewers tied to as many poles; some tied buffalo heads [24] or even guns [25] to the skewers and danced with the objects dangling around them; and there were some who led shying horses by the skewers and thongs.[26]

To end by tearing out the skewer was considered the most efficient way to terminate the dance. Wallis records two accounts by Indian informants concerning days of torture. One man, a Wahpeton at Portage La Prairie, said that he had seen a dancer insert a stick under the flesh on either side of the sternum, fasten the stick to a pole with a thong, and dance for four nights and three days. After freeing himself by tearing out the flesh, he appeared to have his full strength and vigor.[27] According to a second report, another dancer, after four days and four nights, tore out the skewer, took the sweat bath and, after a meal, declared his intention of leading a war party.[28] Walker states that if the Oglala dancers had not "escaped" by the dawn of the next day they were freed from their bonds.[29] The rules allowed brief intermissions during the dance.

In some cases the dancers wept and prayed [30] during their torture, and in others they were expected to sing or show defiance of pain. It could hardly be said that the participants enjoyed the torture. Two influences no doubt were potent in causing them to endure it. One was the general social approval given to the men who had accomplished the dance. The other was the belief that the dance secured the help of the supernatural powers or that these powers demanded it. Wallis gives reports of misfortunes [31]

[22] Walker, *op. cit.,* p. 93.
[23] Skinner, *The Sun Dance of the Plains-Cree,* p. 291. Wissler, *op. cit.,* p. 263.
[24] Walker, *op. cit.,* p. 117.
[25] Robert Jefferson, in Goddard's *Notes on the Sun Dance of the Cree of Alberta,* p. 308. Skinner, *op. cit.,* p. 292.
[26] *Ibid.*
[27] Wallis, *The Sun Dance of the Canadian Dakota,* p. 330.
[28] *Ibid.,* p. 338.
[29] Walker, *op. cit.,* p. 120.
[30] Skinner, *The Sun Dance of the Plains-Ojibway,* p. 314.
[31] Wallis, *op. cit.,* pp. 337-41.

that befell those who had not kept the vow or obeyed the vision which directed them to make the sacrifice. Supposedly on account of refusal to undertake the dance, the family of one man was struck by lightning, and one man's child died. Two were reported to have died because they had entered the dance without being told to do so by the thunders.[32]

The demonstrations of fortitude through torture were limited almost entirely to men. However, Skinner quotes the following from Miss Paget's *The People of the Plains*:

> The women also underwent certain forms of torture, and these, too, required a great deal of courage. These self-sacrifices on the part of the woman were, properly speaking, memorial offerings for the departed ones. The woman who wished to undergo this suffering had her arms, from the elbow down, slashed with cuts from a sharp knife; this also was done by the medicine men. In the case of the women, the torture was inflicted after they had taken part in the dance. Some women, and men also, would have their hair cut short, as a memorial for their dead. As every Indian was proud of his hair, these offerings, though painless, required great self-sacrifice.[33]

Robert Jefferson reports that various forms of torture were used. Once the master of ceremonies had half of his little finger cut off to fulfill a vow. The description of the torture reads:

> A block of wood was brought in and placed beside the fire. The victim made a little speech, telling how he had promised to do this when his child was sick. The child had died, but he was going to keep his word. Some would not have done so, but he was one who did what he said. He sat down on his crossed legs beside the block and began to sing. He laid his fingers on the block, and an old fellow, with a business-like air, held the hand, while with one sweep of a long heavy cleaver-like knife, he chopped off a piece of the finger. The song stopped when amputation was complete.[34]

Integrity was clearly recognized in various ways. In different rites opportunities were given to challenge the word of any woman or girl who laid claim to a quality of virtue which she did not possess.[35] Regardless of the fundamental motives behind the tortures endured by men in order to fulfill a vow, these tortures could not fail to portray a high ideal of integrity.

Bravery in warfare was no doubt linked with fortitude in the mind of the Indian, but he also conceived it as standing by itself.

[32] *Ibid.*, pp. 337-41.

[33] Skinner, *The Sun Dance of the Plains-Cree*, p. 292.

[34] Robert Jefferson, in Goddard's *Notes on the Sun Dance of the Cree in Alberta*, p. 308. See also Lowie, *Sun Dance of the Hidasta*, p. 427. Wissler, *op. cit.*, p. 267.

[35] Wissler, *op. cit.*, p. 240.

Among the Crow, revenge in war being the motive of the mourner, or whistler, as he was called, the ideal of the warrior was kept constantly before the people. A pair of plain moccasins worn by the whistler had to be "sewed by the wife of a man who had killed and scalped an enemy." [36] When a woman put buffalo tongues into the kettle, "a real scalp was tied to the fork she used in the cooking." [37] The master of ceremonies selected an expert marksman and the best butcher to kill and bring in a buffalo. The best scouts in the camp were sent out to report the return of the hunters. In the ceremony connected with cutting the lodge poles, they simulated an attack on an enemy and had a captive take part in the rites. The young men struck the tree with their coup sticks.[38] Later during the cooking of buffalo tongues women carried "bundles of spoils secured by their husbands from the enemy" and likewise brought in the men's guns and bows.[39] One of the warriors represented his exploits in battle by pretending to kill four or five enemies.[40]

As has already been stated, among the Oglala the one prerequisite for the dancer was recognition for bravery. Among the Plains-Cree some endured the torture of the dance merely to show their bravery.[41] In certain rites Sarsi warriors recited their exploits and acted them out with their wives.[42] A similar recounting of brave deeds was found among the Cree in Alberta.[43] During an intermission for the regular Oglala dancers, a group of tried warriors performed the scalp-staff dance in which a leader waved the scalp on his staff in a symbolic manner.[44]

Without going into further detail the extent of the presentation of military ideals is shown by the fact that, of the nineteen tribes studied by Spier, fifteen had some method of torture, fourteen scouted for the lodge pole tree as an enemy, eight counted coups, and six staged sham battles. The Arapaho sun dance frequently included sham battles or attacks and provided several occasions for the recital of the exploits of warriors.[45]

[36] Lowie, *op. cit.*, p. 22.
[37] *Ibid.*, p. 30.
[38] *Ibid.*, p. 32.
[39] *Ibid.*, p. 44.
[40] *Ibid.*
[41] Skinner, *op. cit.*, p. 291.
[42] Goddard, *Notes on the Sun Dance of the Sarsi*, p. 276.
[43] Goddard, *Notes on the Sun Dance of the Cree in Alberta*, p. 304.
[44] Walker, *op. cit.*, p. 119.
[45] Kroeber, *The Arapaho*, pp. 280-82.

SEXUAL PURITY

In the Blackfoot sun dance a woman holds a very prominent place in the ceremony. Some woman had to qualify for this office. The feeling that the sun dance should be performed each year was so strong that sometimes "public opinion had sufficient force to call out volunteers against their own wills." [46] Reluctance to undertake the sun dance was due to the necessary sacrifice of personal comfort and property. Sometimes during her own illness and sometimes during the illness of a member of her family or sometimes out of gratitude for recovery, a woman would make a vow to be the "medicine woman" at the next sun dance. In order to have her supplications answered, the Blackfoot believed that she must be "industrious, truthful, and, above all, true to her marriage vows." [47] If her prayers had not been answered the cause was attributed to the woman's life, and she was accordingly disqualified to participate in the ceremony. In the course of the sun dance the woman bought a sacred bundle with its ritual which was supposed to possess supernatural power.

In addition to the one who had undertaken to be the medicine woman, others had vowed "to go forward to the tongues," [48] a rite observed in the preparation of the buffalo tongues. After the tongues were distributed to the women, the medicine woman made her declaration by saying:

> Sun, I have been true to my husband ever since I have been with him, and all my life. Help me, for what I say is true. I will skin this tongue without cutting a hole in it or cutting my fingers. [49]

Each woman in turn made this public confession. If, in skinning the tongue any one of them cut her finger or cut a hole in the tongue skin, it was considered a sign that she had lied. She was therefore ordered from the tipi.

In the procession of the fourth day and at the raising of the sun pole, these women again made the same public confession to the sun concerning their fidelity. On the fourth day they usually went further and named men who had made improper advances to them. All were subject to challenge concerning the truth of their statements. However, Wissler observes:

[46] Wissler, *op. cit.*, p. 232.
[47] *Ibid.*, p. 232.
[48] *Ibid.*, p. 235.
[49] *Ibid.*, p. 236.

So far as we could learn, no one now living was ever present when one of these women was challenged.[50]

Such activities gave occasion for bringing out the attitude of the Indian toward these characteristics, an illustration of which is found in a narrative recorded by Wissler:

Once while a medicine woman was sleeping in the sacred tipi during the dancing, a nephew of her husband stole in and made improper advances. Being a good and true woman, like all others who gave the sun dance, she spurned him. Next day she told her husband the whole story. He was very angry. He was not satisfied with the confession she made, but suspected that she must have given the young man some encouragement. So when all the medicine men and women had come into the tipi to rehearse the songs as usual, he made a statement of these suspicions and as he had two wives, he proposed to have them change places.

The medicine men pleaded for the first wife because they believed her innocent, but the husband was obdurate. So the second wife was called in to take the place. Then the first wife said, "It was I who saved this man's life when he was ill. I made the vow to give the sun dance and he got well. I have suffered much in fasting, all for him. Now he disgraces me before all the people. But I will put my virtue to a test. If I am true, I have already acquired power."

She filled a pipe, went outside and, standing now on the east side of the tipi, then on the south, the west, and the north, she addressed the sun. The day was clear, but soon after the woman entered the tipi thunder was heard. A storm came down with hail and blew over many tipis. But in spite of these proofs, her husband was obdurate, and the second wife went on with the ceremony.

Not long after the sun dance the same man became ill again. Finally, as a last resort, he called upon the first wife to save him again. This woman told him to call upon the other woman as he seemed to have so much faith in her. So he died and was properly punished for so unjustly treating his faithful wife.

Among the Crow, in the simulated attack on the lodge-pole tree, the leader, or tree-notcher, had to be an absolutely virtuous woman or "one who had been married in the most honorable manner, that is, by purchase, and who had always remained faithful to her husband."[52] Such a woman, after serving in this capacity, could not remarry if her husband died. The invitation to serve was extended by the offer of a buffalo tongue.

If, in spite of her reputation, she was not perfectly chaste, she would openly confess her deficiency, being afraid to deceive the people, for her

[50] Wissler, *North American Indians of the Plains*, p. 240.
[51] *Ibid.*, pp. 247-48.
[52] Lowie, *op. cit.*, p. 30.

acceptance bore the character of an oath, and deception would bring bad luck on the camp.[53]

In the erection of the lodge the Crow also selected an absolutely virtuous woman to lead the procession of firewood carriers.[54] The claims of both of these women were subject to immediate challenge by the men. Lowie cites an account of one woman who was taunted by her relatives for making false pretensions.[55]

In the Oglala sun dance, the women selected to chop the tree for the lodge pole "should be mothers noted for their industry and hospitality, preferably such as have had kindred slain in war." After serving in this capacity, women were entitled to wear a strip of red paint across the forehead. At the same time maidens were selected to comfort and encourage the dancers in their torture.

Then the herald should loudly call the name of each maiden who,. when called, should stand and declare that she has never had carnal intercourse with a man. Anyone may challenge her declaration. If she is challenged and remains silent, it is considered that she is not a maiden. But she may stand and repeat the declaration and bite a snakeskin or the effigy of a snake. If her challenger is then silent, her declaration is considered true. If the challenge is repeated, the challenger must also bite the snake; but if he does not, it is considered that his challenge is a slander. If he does, then a decision should be held in abeyance until a snake decides by biting the one who gave false testimony, as a snake will surely do.[56]

Then the camp marshal announced in a loud voice the names of those who had passed the test, and later a feast was provided for the maidens.

After raising the sun pole on which were hung images of Iya, the patron god of libertinism, and of Gnaski, the Crazy Buffalo, the patron god of licentiousness, the Oglala engaged in a period of banter and jest of sexual relations "to a degree considered an indignity at other times." Then warriors entered, shot down the images and trampled them, thus driving the obscene gods from the camp.[57] There had already been tied to the fork of the sun pole the fetish of the sun dance (the sacred bundle) with the potency of the buffalo god, the patron of fecundity, generosity, and chastity.[58] This god could then prevail in the camp.

[53] *Ibid.*, p. 31.
[54] *Ibid.*, p. 35.
[55] *Ibid.*, p. 31.
[56] Walker, *op. cit.*, p. 99.
[57] *Ibid.*, pp. 108-10.
[58] *Ibid.*, pp. 84, 110.

In the Sarsi sun dance the woman who made the vow to undertake the ceremony and the woman who made the prayer and offering of the buffalo tongue had to meet the same conditions of faithfulness as the corresponding participants in the Blackfoot dance. During one of the rites the woman who held the tongue said: "Pity me, my father, I have lived faithfully with my husband." [59]

Much less emphasis was placed on sexual control among the men. The Oglala, in particular, required the candidate to pledge that he would refrain from sexual intercourse during the ceremony. In the Crow sun dance, the leader of the expedition to get white clay had to be a virtuous young man. It had to be a man "who had never taken liberties with any woman but his wife and had never played with his sisters-in-law." According to an account given by Wallis, the Canadian Dakota demanded chaste young men for one rite:

The pole which is used may be gotten and set up only by chaste unmarried men. All those who help do this are previously asked if they have had intercourse with women; if they confess to this, they may not participate. This requirement is said to have acted as a strong deterrent on the passions of the young men of the tribe. If one not qualified fails to confess and subsequently participates in the preparation for the ceremony, he will be killed in the next fight. This restraint is now gone, and morals are going too, say the old men. [60]

Various other qualities of character were implied in the sun dance. In addition to rules already mentioned the candidate for shaman in the Oglala dance should refrain from becoming angry and should not hear ribald speech nor go into water during the ceremony. [61] Numerous taboos were enforced, but they dealt mainly with ceremonial procedure and had little to do with social virtues apart from the rituals. The Blackfoot medicine woman and her husband were put to bed in their tipi by her father and mother. The next morning the parents gave the son and the daughter a small amount of food and then ate a little themselves. [62] In this manner, they put into practice one of the teachings of Hako. [63] During the fasting period the Blackfoot showed their respect for the medicine woman by remaining quiet while

[59] Goddard, *Notes on the Sun Dance of the Sarsi*, pp. 275, 278.
[60] Wallis, *The Sun Dance of the Canadian Dakota*, p. 326.
[61] Walker, *op. cit.*, p. 71.
[62] Wissler, *The Sun Dance of the Blackfoot Indians*, p. 242.
[63] Fletcher, *The Hako, A Pawnee Religious Ceremony*, p. 117.

in her tipi, by keeping down noises in the vicinity, and by abstaining from boisterous acts throughout the camp.[64]

CROW MILITARY SOCIETIES

One of the outstanding characteristics of the Indians of the Plains was the tendency to organize into societies. Purposes and regulations varied in these organizations, but practically all of them set up certain standards to which the individual was to conform. In the dancing societies of the Sarsi, whose activities were largely social, the candidate applied for membership and secured it through purchase.[65] In the age societies of the Hidasta and the Mandan, each group successively made a collective purchase of the society from an older group.[66] The Pawnee societies stressed religious rites and helped to preserve their traditions.[67] Some Blackfoot societies [68] had military and police functions with standards resembling those of the Crow. Certain Oglala societies had special military requirements for the conduct of officers.[69] Arikara societies seem to have been largely social; some served as police or guards, and the main object of one society was to aid the poor.[70] In his introduction to a volume on the *Societies of the Plains Indians*, Wissler says:

The three characteristics of Plains societies to impress early observers were their police and soldier functions, age qualifications, and no-flight obligations. While these are by no means universal, they are nevertheless valid characters. The first is so nearly universal that we have taken it as a convenient means of departure.

After discussing the variety of organizations that had been found by anthropologists, Wissler continues:

Yet a glance through these pages will reveal the essential unity of subject matter, for many societies can be traced along from first to last leaving no room for doubt that we are here dealing with the same organizations.[71]

With the understanding that the Crow laid more than average stress on military features, the descriptions which follow may be taken as fairly representative of their type.

[64] Wissler, *op. cit.*, p. 242.
[65] Goddard, *Dancing Societies of the Sarsi Indians*, p. 465.
[66] Lowie, *Societies of the Hidasta and Mandan Indians*, pp. 225, 294.
[67] Murie, *Pawnee Societies*, pp. 561-67.
[68] Wissler, *Societies and Dance Associations of the Blackfoot Indians*, p. 370.
[69] Wissler, *Societies and Ceremonial Associations in the Oglala Division of the Teton-Dakota*, pp. 15-27.
[70] Lowie, *Societies of the Arikara Indians*, pp. 661, 662, 664.
[71] Wissler, Introduction to *Societies of the Plains Indians*, VI.

In the Crow military societies we find permanent self-organized groups within the tribe. While military features were prominent, though probably not fundamental, Lowie regards the societies as clubs:

... associations held together by a strong band of comradeship, the members helping one another as the occasion arose and meeting frequently for purely social purpose.

In contrast with the ceremonial procedures that have been discussed, Crow military societies were not religious agencies.[72] They also showed a different attitude toward the individual. In the sun dance the tribe joined in the accomplishment of the purposes of individuals. In most of the Crow military societies the organized group sought the individual and offered him the inducement of a share in its purposes. Usually members joined at the request of the society to take the place of a deceased relative.

Lowie's account makes a very satisfactory basis for study because his own investigations were carried on in the light of previous records. Historically he introduces his report as follows:

For convenience' sake the societies that form the subject of this paper may be collectively referred to as "military societies." The earliest reference to them dates back to 1804, when Lewis and Clark discovered a Dakota Society of men pledged to foolhardy conduct and learned that this was organized in imitation of the societies of the Crow. Probably about two decades later, Beckworth noted the existence of the rival Dog and Fox societies. In 1833 Maximilian enumerated eight Crow organizations—the Bulls, Prairie-Foxes, Ravens, Half-Shaved Heads, Lumpwoods, Stone Hammers, Little Dogs, and Big Dogs. When I first visited the Crow in 1907, I learned of only four societies of this type, Foxes, Lumpwoods, Big Dogs, and Muddy Hands. These are likewise the only ones described by Mr. Curtis in his recent work, though he refers in addition, without giving names, to boys' organizations modeled on those of the older men. Persistent inquiry among practically all old Crow informants enabled me, however, to obtain, not only all the names of Maximilian's list but also two or three additional ones.[73]

It should be noted that some of Lowie's informants in 1910 were about ninety years of age, giving information that can be considered reliable for conditions as far back as 1840.[74] Further, he checked his results carefully with similar societies in neighboring tribes for borrowings and interpretations.

[72] Lowie. *op. cit.*, p. 150.
[73] *Ibid.*, p. 147.
[74] *Ibid.*, p. 153.

By reason of their large membership and mutual rivalry, the Foxes and the Lumpwoods furnish the best examples for special study. Their greatest moral teachings are found in the duties of their officers and in the regulations recognized by the two societies in their contests and other relationships.

The origin of the Fox organization was attributed to visions or dreams.[75] The organization was divided into several groups. The youngest members, boys about eighteen or twenty years of age, were called the "Bad Ones" because of their noise, play, and jokes. The "Little Foxes" were about thirty years old, and the "Foxes proper were quiet, good-humored men of mature age." [76] Two older men, selected by the boys, stayed with them as they sat together in the society's lodge. The younger members were allowed freedom to romp and play jokes.[77] Other subdivisions known to some informants have little significance for our purpose.

The origin of the Lumpwoods was accounted for in various ways. Lowie says:

According to Hunts-to-die, the Indians of long ago divided into two parties for a kicking-game. The two sides got angry at each other and began to steal each other's wives. One division, the later Lumpwoods, made an emblem composed of a knobbed club about four feet long, whence their name. Pretty-enemy said that the Lumpwoods were originally called Half-shaved Heads, but that on one war expedition a member carrying a knobbed club struck the first coup, and accordingly the entire society changed its name in honor of his weapon.[78]

Similar versions give different explanations for their development. None, however, is more adequate than the explanation in the passage quoted. The Lumpwoods also had subdivisions which apparently had no special significance.

A particular feature of the Lumpwoods was their custom of making jokes at the expense of one another, a practice which originated with the Big Dogs. It was a custom especially in favor when a member had lost a relative. It seemed to be more common when a half-witted member of the family had died. Nevertheless, the practice was employed after the death of others as well, and must have been intended to prevent the bereaved from mourning too long or from thinking too much about the dead.[79]

[75] *Ibid.*, p. 156.
[76] *Ibid.*
[77] *Ibid.*, p. 157.
[78] *Ibid.*, p. 163.
[79] *Ibid.*, pp. 167-68.

The interests of the Foxes and the Lumpwoods concentrated no little on their mutual relations. Lowie says that the feeling of rivalry was quite free from any personal hostility.[80] Their competition showed itself in games, in attempts to steal the wives of members of the rival society, and especially in the comparison of their war records.

Regardless of what may have been the reasons for the practice, the stealing of wives called for a high degree of self-control on the part of the one who sustained the loss. According to the rules followed, on certain occasions a member of one society could steal the wife of a member of the other organization, if he had had relations with her as her paramour before her marriage. The stealing took place after it was duly announced. Neither the woman nor her husband was allowed to offer any resistance to the kidnapper or to behave in an unfriendly way.[81] The husband was not even supposed to show any sorrow. Both the woman and her husband lost prestige if they failed to maintain the proper attitudes. The rival society often destroyed their opponents' property as a method of reprisal or composed songs to ridicule their competitors.[82] Nothing could demonstrate more effectively the control which public opinion exercised through the organized approval or disapproval of a group.

After kidnapping the wives who were subject to capture, the Foxes and the Lumpwoods would go on the warpath and keep scores of their exploits.

Before entering battle, warriors composed songs to sing in commemoration of their expected victory. In case one society was surpassed by the other in warlike deeds against the enemy, the members of the victorious group stole the songs of their rivals and substituted words of ridicule.

The influence of this rivalry may be seen in an incident in an attack on the enemy, as recorded by Lowie:

A Fox Hook-staff officer went up some distance, but then lay down with his standard. A brave member of the Lumpwood rank and file asked, "Has anyone struck the enemy yet?" "No, it is pretty difficult." Then the Lumpwood snatched away the Fox officer's pole, went up the hill, and struck an enemy with it. He left the standard over a hole on the butte, ran back, reached his people in safety, and challenged the Foxes to recover

[80] Lowie, *Societies of the Arikara Indians*, p. 169.
[81] *Ibid.*, p. 169.
[82] *Ibid.*, p. 174.

their emblem. None of them dared go for it. When the party came back from the war, the Lumpwoods took away the Foxes' songs. In such a case, the Foxes were obliged to borrow the songs of other societies. Red-eye gave me the following song composed by Lumpwoods in derision of the Foxes when a hooked-staff officer ran away from the enemy: "You Foxes, you ran away fast. A man must die anyway." [83]

Thus not only the shame of defeat but systematized ridicule awaited the vanquished warriors.

This same compulsion through social pressure characterized the selection of officers in the two societies through which their military attitudes were clearly shown. As officers the Foxes had "two leaders, two men with hooked staffs wrapped with otterskin, two men bearing straight staffs similarly wrapped, two rear or 'last' men, and one or two akducire." [84] The akducire were expected to show the greatest bravery and incur the greatest risks. In recognition of these dangers, they were honored by permission to select the food they wished at feasts and to eat before the others began. Staff officers in battle "were expected to plant their staffs in the ground, and stay by their standards at the risk of their lives." [85] In retreat the officers were expected to dismount and resist the enemy.[86]

All the officers were highly honored. Among other distinctions during the dances, the four staff officers were permitted to turn their backs to the rest in a way not permitted to other members. In spite of the honors, however, it was difficult to induce men to accept the position. They looked upon their officers as "doomed to die." [87] Here again the Crow used social pressure to secure the ends desired by the group. At the meeting for the annual election of their leaders, several old men would remain outside to discuss who would make good officers. After deciding on two leaders, they would come in and offer them the pipe. If the chosen two refused to smoke the pipe, it was offered to others. Sometimes the honor was declined by each member. If this happened, more strenuous means were adopted. Lowie gives Young-jack-rabbit's account of his election in the Lumpwoods who followed the same practice:

[83] *Ibid.*, p. 175.
[84] *Ibid.*, p. 158.
[85] *Ibid.*
[86] *Ibid.*, p. 161.
[87] *Ibid.*, p. 157.

All declined to smoke, then they came towards me. Someone asked them "Whom are you looking for?" They answered, "For Young-jack-rabbit." I was seated in the back and tried to hide. They brought the pipe to me, but I refused to accept it, saying I did not wish to take it. One of the pipe-offerers was my own elder brother. He seized me by the hair, hit me on the chest, and said, "You are brave, why don't you smoke the pipe?" He wished me to die, that is why he desired me to smoke the pipe. He said, "You are of the right age to die; you are good-looking; and if you get killed your friends will cry. All your relatives will cut their hair, they will fast and mourn; your bravery will be recognized; and your friends will feel gratified." I took the pipe, and began to smoke. They asked me, whether I wished to have a straight or hooked-staff. I decided in favor of the latter. My comrade also smoked the pipe. . . . We all went outside, the leaders in front. An old man slapped me on the chest, saying, "Now you are a brave man. When the enemy pursue, you must get off and keep them back. If you are willing to do this, dance backwards when we have a dance." I dressed up in my best clothes. That day I thought I looked handsome. The old men sang songs in praise of me.[88]

After the election of officers the Foxes marched through the camp to honor their new leaders. Otterskins were provided for their poles by the parents of the staff-bearers. At the staff-bearer's lodge a former officer who had carried the stick recounted his warlike deeds and said:

I should like you to do the same that I did and strike the enemy. We know you are a brave man. We wish you to fight for your people.[89]

Both the Foxes and the Lumpwoods held ceremonies in honor of the deceased members.[90] On such occasions some gashed their faces, and others wounded themselves with arrows. Among the Lumpwoods, if the younger men hesitated to cut themselves, the officers did it for them.

The Crow had several other societies of less influence. Frequently Foxes or Lumpwoods belonged to other societies as well. Among the Big Dogs, two officers were expected "to walk straight up to the enemy regardless of danger and never to retreat."[91] After the death of a member in battle, the Big Dogs paraded through the camp in his honor. The parents or the wife of the slain man led his horse toward the men. "Whoever mounted the horse pledged himself to act like the dead man and to be so brave as to be killed."[92]

[88] Lowie, *Societies of the Arikara Indians*, p. 166.
[89] *Ibid.*, p. 161.
[90] *Ibid.*, pp. 162, 166.
[91] *Ibid.*, p. 177.
[92] *Ibid.*, p. 180.

When the Crow were retreating in battle, Big Dog officers could flee with them; but, if they heard a cry for help from a fellow-tribesman, two of their officers were expected to "rush to the rescue at the risk of their lives." [93]

The akducire were expected to die, no matter what happened. To return alive was to become the laughingstock of their fellow-tribesmen. Graybull recalled a number of akducire who had been killed in battle, but not a single one that had acted in a cowardly manner.[94]

In declining an office members would sometimes make the very frank admission that they were cowards and afraid to die.[95]

The "Hammer Society" was composed of boys. They elected their officers after the manner of the men's organizations. Their akducire were expected to be as fearless before animals as those of the men's societies were before the enemy.[96] Sometimes older men became members and joined war parties. At the performance in honor of a dead comrade two men, urged by the slain warrior's father, pledged themselves to avenge the death of their friend. Both came out alive.[97]

Members of some of the societies served as police. Other societies, such as that of the Crazy-dogs-wishing-to-die, had special purposes. This society was composed of men who had become tired of life. They were expected to seek death deliberately by running into danger for one season at least.

The negative aspects of control through social approval and disapproval may be illustrated by the Bull Society, composed of men fifty or sixty years of age. In ceremonies two of their officers wore masks of buffalo heads and were considered foolhardy, "made to die." [98] Buffalo tails were worn by those who had dismounted in battle. They made great pretensions in their public dances, snorting, pawing, bellowing, and charging the spectators. In spite of all this, Lowie reports the following:

They always bore themselves well in battle until a certain engagement north of Pryor, when they were driven down a low cliff, whence they were called "Bulls-chased-over-the-cliff." The mockery thus incurred put a stop to the society.[99]

[93] *Ibid.*, p. 181.
[94] *Ibid.*, p. 187.
[95] *Ibid.*, p. 181.
[96] *Ibid.*, p. 187.
[97] *Ibid.*, p. 188.
[98] *Ibid.*, p. 189.
[99] *Ibid.*, p. 189.

Nothing could demonstrate more effectively the influence of public opinion systematically directed toward the attainment of certain ends. Ordinarily warriors could retreat without being disgraced but not after such pretensions.

THE VIRTUES TAUGHT IN THE SUN DANCE AND IN MILITARY SOCIETIES

In considering the moral values in the sun dance and in military societies, we should conceive education as the transmission of ideals of conduct with an effort to make those ideals prevail. From this point of view, our problem may be stated, thus: What ideas did the sun dance and military societies transmit? How did they transmit these ideas?

Whether or not the participants in the sun dance were conscious of the fact that they were transmitting ideas, it is quite clear that they were endeavoring to make their ideals prevail. Attendance was largely compulsory. A prescribed ceremonial had to be followed. People were taught that wrong methods would bring misfortune to the tribe, and it was thought that the supernatural powers would punish those who refused to undertake the sun dance when directed to do so. Any participant who neglected the regular forms was, as a rule, ejected at once. It is quite clear that the participants in the sun dance were consciously preserving ceremonial procedure and enforcing the observance of the proper rites.

Though it was not so evident, they must also have been conscious of the fact that they were teaching the great virtues. It should be recalled that both children and adults knew what took place in the village, even in places where attendance at the sun dance was not compulsory. It is not likely that children missed many of the spectacular activities of the adults. The sun dance, then, was an open book for all the members of the tribe. In it they could read the great motives that stirred the people to action and to sacrifice. In it they could see the great virtues honored.

Their ideas of warfare were portrayed through sham battles, the recounting of exploits and the dramatization of brave deeds, the revenge sought by some pledgers, and the qualities required of many of the participants. The distribution of gifts and provision for feasts demonstrated the generosity of the pledgers and their friends. There was no need of a theoretical discussion of fortitude. Fortitude itself was presented and honored. The ideal of integrity was shown by the significance attached to the individual's word. False pretensions were challenged and brought ridicule and disgrace. The Indian kept his word by the flow of his own blood.

The qualities most highly respected in women were not neglected. In many tribes the sun dance itself was undertaken by the people to fulfill the vow of a woman who was solicitous for the health of her family. Those who had preserved their sexual purity were singled out for positions of unusual distinction in the ceremony and were afterwards highly honored for their virtuous life. The place of woman's work in the life of the village was displayed in many of the functions which she performed in the course of the various rites.

While individuals possessing these virtues were exhibited to the people with great esteem and honor, the virtues themselves were not forced upon any member of the group. It is true that those who lacked certain qualities were not permitted to perform some of the rites. Yet the absence of the virtues exhibited did not bring on disgrace. There was considerable laxity in sexual relations. Aside from those in certain positions of honor, no one assumed any obligations committing him to a particular type of moral conduct. The sun dance presented the great virtues to the individual with all the force of tribal approval behind them, but it left to him the decision as to whether he adopted them or not.

In this attitude, the Indian possessed a certain degree of freedom. The sun dance did not set up any machinery for the purpose of enforcing its teachings. Participation in the ceremony itself demonstrated a high regard for the personality of the individual. While the sun dance was thought to have a value for the whole tribe, it was undertaken by all for the accomplishment of the purposes of an individual or of individuals. In other words, in the celebration of the sun dance the people showed their respect for the personality of those who had made the vow to undertake it. In a sense they all shared in the purposes and aspirations of the pledgers.

This point of view leads to a contrast with the Crow military societies. Through a feeling of obligation to a deceased relative and through gifts and social pressure, the military society drew the individual as an aid in accomplishing its purposes. After the individual became a member, the society often practically forced him to take an office that meant almost certain death. The members recognized this fact when they spoke of their officers as "doomed to die." On account of the practical nature of some of its functions, the military society devised means for the concentration of social approval and scorn by which its standard of conduct was enforced.

The great virtue taught by the military societies was bravery in warfare. Yet the highest type of bravery was required only of the officer. He was clearly and consciously sacrificed for the good of the group. He might decline the honor on the plea that he was afraid to die, but when he had once assumed the obligation he had to stand his ground. The effectiveness of the military society's method of teaching is proved by the fact that a lack of proper conduct among officers was almost unknown. The loud and pretentious Bull Society was broken up by a disgraceful retreat before the enemy.

Among the military societies, wife-stealing could not have had much, if any, ethical value. It seemed to be the blind following of a custom kept alive, through rivalry and the feeling of obligation, for the purpose of observing the regulations. On the other hand, even in this practice, which many Indians deplored, chastity was respected. The woman who had had no paramour before her marriage was not subject to capture. A knowledge of this fact no doubt restrained young women in their conduct and influenced young men in the matter of selecting their wives.

The military societies were mutually-respecting units within the tribe. In warfare and in their mutual rivalries, they taught that the game of life should be played according to rules. Such relationships implied toleration of opinions and attitudes of others.

In spite of their defects, the military societies developed or adopted standards of conduct and enforced acceptance of these standards among their members. They knew what situations it would take to secure the responses desired. They probably utilized the individual's reactions to social approval and scorn more effectively than did any other primitive organization. Combining the spectacular and the sacred, the sun dance made an appeal to the supernatural throughout the ceremony. The military society of the Crow made no appeal to religious motives. For results it depended entirely upon human factors.

CHAPTER V

MORAL TEACHINGS IN THE HAKO, A PAWNEE RELIGIOUS CEREMONY

In the arrangement and congruity of ideas, Tlingit myths represent one extreme of our study, and the Hako of the Pawnee represent the other. While it is true that numerous elements of environment and various aspects of conduct had become subjects for thought and reflection among the Tlingit, their ideas lacked the organization and unity that characterized Pawnee philosophy. The Tlingit believed in spirits that individuals could control, but they did not express in any systematic way their more or less hazy conceptions of supernatural powers. The wonderful transformations recounted in their myths were naïvely attributed to magic; at the same time, few explanations were given or deemed necessary upon the subject of the ultimate source of such power or the methods by which such miracles were performed. With the exception of funeral rites and the magical practices of shamans and medicine men, they seem to have had no distinctly religious ceremony that corresponded to Pawnee worship.

In the Hako, on the other hand, the universe was conceived as being controlled by some degree of law and order. The Pawnee developed a fairly consistent system of theology. One mighty supernatural power and numerous subordinate powers were regarded as the maker, the guardians, the protectors of the world, animal life, and the human race. A knowledge of their religious rites and many of their virtues was attributed to the guidance of the powers above or to revelations made by them. Their religious ideas and practices, their symbolic appeal to the supernatural, their most important family and social virtues were all worked into an elaborate combination of rites, prayers, and songs which, though unaided by written language, possessed an indisputable richness, unity, and harmony. Such a combination was the Hako.

The basis for this study is "The Hako, a Pawnee Ceremony," by Miss Alice C. Fletcher. At her request, Tahirussawichi, a full-blood Pawnee, reproduced all of the songs and rituals, giving at each step detailed explanations concerning their significance to the Indian.   Graphophone records were made of the songs, from which the music was transcribed by Edwin S. Tracy.   Through the assistance of James R. Murie, an educated Pawnee, Miss Fletcher translated the texts into English.   Several years elapsed before the whole task was finished.   While Tahirussawichi and Mr. Murie were her guests in Washington in 1898 and in 1900 and during her visits to the Pawnee in 1899 and in 1901, Miss Fletcher and Mr. Murie were engaged in recording and translating the rituals.   The report was published in 1904.[1]

The extent to which the Hako was used is difficult to determine. Miss Fletcher witnessed it several times in the Omaha tribe "in the early eighties of the last century."[2]   She thinks that the feathered stems, sacred objects used in the Hako, were seen by Marquette in 1672:

> Marquette calls the feathered stem a "calumet," and his description of its ceremony, which he saw among the Illinois, due allowance being made for his lack of intimate acquaintance with native religious customs, indicated that the ceremony as he saw it over two hundred years ago in a tribe that no longer exists differs little from the same ceremony as observed within the last twenty years in the Omaha tribe.

> He says of this calumet that it is "the most mysterious thing in the world.   The scepters of our kings are not so much respected, for the Indians have such a reverence for it that one may call it the god of peace and war and the arbiter of life and death. . . .   One with this calumet may venture among his enemies, and in the hottest battles they lay down their arms before the sacred pipe.   The Illinois presented me with one of them which was very useful to us in our voyage."[3]

THE PAWNEE

The Pawnee Nation was composed of four tribes or bands [4]— the Chau-i, "in the middle"; the Kit-ke-hahk-i, "on a hill"; the Pita-hau-erat, "down the stream"; and the Skidi, or "wolf."   The same bands were also, respectively, the Grand, the Republican, the Tapage, and the Wolf Pawnee.[5]   They belonged to the Caddoan family,[6] which included the Arikara, to the north, and the Caddo,

[1] Fletcher, *The Hako, A Pawnee Religious Ceremony*, pp. 14-16.
[2] *Ibid.*, p. 13.
[3] *Ibid.*, p. 279.
[4] Grinnell, *Pawnee Hero Stories and Folk-Tales*, pp. 215-16.
[5] *Handbook of American Indians*, Vol. II, p. 215.
[6] Dunbar, *Magazine of American History*, Vol. IV, p. 241.   *Handbook of American Indians*, Vol. II, p. 214.

the Waco, the Kichai, the Tawakoni, and the Pawnee Pict or Wichita to the south.

In 1875, the Pawnee sold their land to the United States Government and moved to a reservation in Oklahoma.[7] Until this date, from the time when they became acquainted with the whites, their permanent home had been on the Platte and the Loup rivers in southern Nebraska and in northern Kansas. They had two traditions concerning their migrations.[8] In the older account, they came from the southwest, possibly from old Mexico. According to the newer story, they had lived in Louisiana and Mississippi, indicating no doubt the lines which their movements had followed.

In southern Nebraska, they engaged in a long struggle with and finally conquered the Ponca, the Omaha, and the Oto, who afterwards lived on the border of Pawnee ground, nominally under their protection.[9] The Dakota (the Sioux) to the north, the Crow, in the more distant northwest, and the Comanche and Osage somewhat to the south "were avowed foes"[10] of the Pawnee. These conditions forced the Pawnee to maintain the warlike spirit which characterized most of the Indians. Dunbar, in 1880, said: "The Pawnee were in instinct and history thoroughly warlike."[11] Grinnell, from visits with them from 1870 to 1889, observed: "The Pawnees were a race of warriors. War was their pleasure and business. By war they gained credit, respect, fame. By war they acquired wealth."[12] Frequent attacks by the Sioux and Cheyenne kept the Pawnee ever ready to mount his steed and dash out to defend his home. The Sioux would sometimes come in superior numbers, but the Pawnee practically always drove them back because they knew that the lives of their families were at stake.

Early in their relations with the whites they made treaties of peace which caused them to be considered more or less the allies of the whites against their common enemies. Many of their warriors enlisted under the United States Government as scouts and served with great distinction. Their attitude toward the whites undoubtedly added to the hosility which their fierce neighbors nurtured against them.

[7] *Ibid.*
[8] Grinnell, *op. cit.*, p. 334.
[9] Grinnell, *op. cit.*, pp. 304-05. Dunbar. *Magazine of American History*, Vol. IV, p. 252.
[10] Dunbar, *Magazine of American History*, Vol. V, p. 334.
[11] *Ibid.*
[12] Grinnell, *op. cit.*, p. 303.

The inevitable result of life under such conditions was a gradual decrease in population. According to Dunbar, the Pawnee numbered 12,500 in 1834; 8,400 in 1847; 4,686 in 1856; 3,416 in 1861; and 1,440 in 1879.[13] In 1889 they numbered 800.[14]

Though the Pawnee raised beans, the squash, and the pumpkin, they were widely known for their cultivation of corn which, with buffalo meat, constituted their main source of food.[15] They traced their use of corn to the powers above who gave it to the people soon after they began life in this world. Their recognition of its value will be shown by the place of honor which they gave to Mother Corn in the ceremonies.

PAWNEE TRADITIONS

From Grinnell, Dorsey, and Murie, apart from the teachings of the Hako, may be gathered a fairly consistent account of Pawnee beliefs in regard to the creation of the world and the influence of supernatural powers.

"In the beginning was Tirawahut (the Universe-and-Everything-Inside)"[16] presided over by the All-Powerful Tiráwa with his spouse Atira (Vault-of-the-sky). Tiráwa assigned the gods to their places—The Sun, Moon, Bright-Star (Evening-Star), Great-Star (Morning-Star), North-Star (Star-that-does-not-move), and the Spirit-Star in the south. Other stars were stationed in the northeast, the northwest, the southwest, and the southeast to touch the earth with their feet and to hold up the heavens with their hands. The earth was not yet made. Bright-Star had a beautiful garden below the heavens. Tiráwa told Bright-Star that he would send gods to her—Clouds, Winds, Lightnings, and Thunders—and that when she placed them between her and her garden they would turn to human beings. Tiráwa then said that he was ready to make the earth. Through these gods the land and water were divided. Then timber and underbrush appeared and were later given life by the Winds, the Rains, the Lightnings, and the Thunders, who also dropped seeds on the land to take root.

A boy was born to Sun and Moon, and Great-Star and Bright-Star became parents of a girl. The Clouds were instructed to take

13 Dunbar, *Magazine of American History*, Vol. IV, p. 254.
14 Grinnell, *op. cit.*, p. 10.
15 *Ibid.*, pp. 253-54.
16 Dorsey, *Traditions of the Skidi Pawnee*, pp. 3-5.

the boy and girl to the earth. Here they wandered until they found each other. They did not seem to know anything or to care for anything until a child was born to them. Then they "seemed to understand all; that they must labor to feed the child and to clothe him." [17] In time the gods brought various gifts to help the people in providing food and clothing.

At first, human beings on the earth were immortal; death had not appeared. One of the stars became jealous and sent Wolf to the earth. After an encounter with human beings, Wolf was killed, thus bringing death into the world. Secret Pipe Chief, a high priest, told Grinnell [18] that they believed that after death the good would live again with Tiráwa in the sky. He gave as evidence the fact that they had dreamed of being with Tiráwa. He maintained that he himself had lived on the earth before. In a number of stories,[19] the existence of the spirits of the dead and human communication with them are taken for granted. In the stories [20] of the Ghost Wife and the Ghost Bride, each woman returned to earth after death. One of them tried to persuade her husband to go back with her, saying: "There is a place to go where we would not be unhappy."

In the first lodge occupied by human beings, an altar was placed on the west side to be kept holy. After the number of families had increased and were occupying several tents, the man, following directions from Bright-Star, tanned the hide of a yellow female buffalo calf and wrapped in this covering the holy corn, "the flint-stone, the skins of owls, hawks, paints, pipe, tobacco, and sweet grass." [21] These articles, hung up in the lodge, composed the holy bundle. According to Grinnell,[22] the lodge of every Pawnee preserved a similar bundle.

GOVERNMENT AND SOCIAL ORGANIZATIONS

We are told by Murie that the sacred bundle determined very largely the form of government and social organization, especially among the Skidi. The chiefs inherited their positions although, in filling vacancies, the older men exercised some judgment in selecting new chiefs from the families of the deceased. There was

17 Dorsey, *op. cit.*, p. 7.
18 Grinnell, *op. cit.*, p. 355.
19 Dorsey, *op. cit.*, pp. 69-79.
20 Grinnell, *op cit.*, pp. 129-31, 191-94.
21 Dorsey, *op. cit.*, p. 9.
22 Grinnell, *op. cit.*, p. 351.

a chief for each sacred bundle, but a priest had particular charge of the bundle and its rituals. The office of priest was hereditary, and the position of chief priest was held for a year in rotation by the priests of the village.

This chief priest is the highest authority; he is the source of the final appeal, and to him all acts of the council of chiefs must be referred. The buffalo hunt in particular must be regulated according to the ritual of the bundle whose priest happens to be in charge.[23]

These special sacred bundles belonged to various military or hunting societies whose rituals served to keep alive many Pawnee traditions and to intensify their religious fervor. Admission to these organizations, however, was secured through election. Although they had a limited membership, many of their ceremonies were performed in public. The sacrifice of smoke to Tiráwa, symbolic dances, a recounting of stories connected with the sacred bundle, instructions as to how to proceed, and a prayer for success in the hunt were the main features of these ceremonies. None of them approached the Hako in the breadth of its interests or in the value of the ideals which it endeavored to instill. Nevertheless, these features do show that the Hako does not misrepresent the deeply religious spirit of the Pawnee and the poetic symbolism which permeated their life and thought.

PURPOSE AND SCHEME OF THE HAKO

In contrast with the societies just mentioned, the Hako was not a permanent organization with a definite membership or a definite time or particular motive for its celebration. It was simply an intertribal religious ceremony which required the coöperation of a large number of individuals for a period of several days. It was a "prayer for children, in order that the tribe may increase and be strong; and also that the people may have long life, enjoy plenty, and be happy and at peace." [24]

The participants [25] were divided into two groups, the Fathers and the Children, representing two different clans or gentes of a tribe or of two different tribes. The exchange of gifts and other expenses made it necessary for the Fathers to be drawn from the wealthier members of the community. The organizer of this group, called the Father, was a man of wealth and prominence, if

[23] Murie, *Pawnee Indian Societies*, p. 554.
[24] Fletcher, *op. cit.*, p. 26.
[25] *Ibid.*, pp. 18-19.

not a chief. As the presence of a chief was essential in the rituals, two chiefs were always included in the party. From the number of those who knew the rites and songs, the Father had to select one man to be supervisor and director of the entire ceremony. This man was called Kúrahus, which was a title given to a venerable man "instructed in the meaning and use of sacred objects as well as their ceremonies." [26] The Kúrahus, or leader of the ceremony, was accompanied by an assistant and by an apprentice. A priest, two doctors, and a number of singers, together with the kindred and contributing friends of the Father, completed his party.

The ceremony required that the Son, the leader of the Children should be a man of equal rank with the Father. The Son and the Children, as already stated, were to be of a different clan. Frequently they belonged to a different tribe. Various rituals were sung during the preparation of the sacred objects in the Father's lodge, during the Son's journey to the village, and at his lodge where, open to the public, the greater part of the ceremony took place. No attempt has been made to present a consecutive account in this chapter. The teaching of particular ideas or virtues can readily be shown by selecting the rituals in which they appear. Many of the rituals were complete in themselves.

THE THEOLOGY OF THE HAKO

The main religious conceptions of the Pawnee are stated clearly in the explanations of the Kúrahus concerning the songs sung in the making of the sacred objects and in various symbolic activities of the ceremony. In summary form, the Indian's point of view may be given as follows: Above us, far away in the blue, silent sky, there is a holy place to which prayers may be sent and from which help comes to men. They speak of this place with reverence. It is the abode of the mighty Tiráwa, the father of all, the maker of all things, the giver of life to man.

All the powers that are in the heavens and all those that are upon the earth are derived from the mighty power, Tiráwa atius. He is the father of all the lesser powers, those which can approach man. He is the father of all the people and perpetuates the life of the tribe through the gift of children. So we sing, your father meaning the father of all people everywhere, the father of all things that we see and hear and feel. [27]

[20] *Ibid.*, p. 15.
[27] *Ibid.*, p. 107.

As we sing these words over and over we think about Tiráwa atius being the father of all things. . . .

The white man speaks of a heavenly Father; we say Tiráwa atius, the Father above, but we do not think of Tiráwa as a person. We think of Tiráwa as in everything, as the power which has arranged and thrown down from above everything that man needs. What the power above, Tiráwa atius, is like, no one knows; nc one has been there.[28]

Lesser Powers. Tiráwa atius, the mighty power, cannot approach men directly. He sends help through the lesser powers who can be seen and felt by them. The lesser powers [29] dwell in the blue dome of the sky, below the abode of Tiráwa atius. The first among the lesser powers are the invisible Winds, the breath of Tiráwa, giving life to man; they stand at the four directions as guards over the paths along which the lesser powers bring their aid to men. The other lesser powers are visible. The Sun comes directly from the mighty Tiráwa and brings vitality, strength, and growth. They also pray to the Earth as mother, a resting place and the source of food; to forms of Vegetation, which supply food and clothing; to Water, essential to the life of man and plants. "The Winds, the Sun, the Earth, the Vegetation, and the Water are the five lesser powers through which the life of our bodies is maintained." [30]

Visions and Dreams. In the sky below the dwelling place of the lesser powers is found the abode of visions which bring messages to men.

When a vision is sent by the powers, it descends to the person designated, who sees the vision and hears what it has to say; then, as day approaches, the vision ascends to its dwelling place, Katasha, and there it lies at rest until it is called again.[31]

Spirits of Birds and Plants. The spirits of birds and plants also mediate between the powers of the heavens and men. The eagle soars aloft, reaching even the abode of the lesser powers.[32] The spirit of Mother Corn ascends to the circle of the lesser powers, from whom she gets authority to lead in the ceremony.[33] They regard the eagle as chief of the day; the owl, of the night; the woodpecker, of the trees; the duck, of the water.[34]   Parts

[28] Fletcher, *The Hako, A Pawnee Religious Ceremony,* p. 216.
[29] *Ibid.,* p. 29.
[30] *Ibid.,* p. 32.
[31] *Ibid.,* p. 155.
[32] *Ibid.,* pp. 99, 125.
[33] *Ibid.,* p. 46.
[34] *Ibid.,* p. 40.

of these birds were fastened to the feathered stem to symbolize the presence of their spirits, whose movements through the air to seek the aid of Tiráwa were to be as swift as the flight of the birds themselves.

Origin and Value of Ceremony. The Indians believed that long ago the powers above revealed to their fathers, through visions, how to make the sacred objects of the Hako and how to conduct the entire ceremony.

All the good, all the happiness that comes to those who take part in these rites have been promised in a dream, and the dreams which brought this ceremony and its promises came from the east; they always descend from above by that path.[35]

On the side of values, while the correct performance of the rites of the Hako were considered as a means to gain favor from above, one is impressed with the great significance attached to moral conduct. According to the explanations of the Kúrahus, the leader : "The teachings of this ceremony make a straight line along which if a man walks he will receive help from the powers." [36]

Methods of Transmitting Moral and Religious Ideas. Most of the ideas previously mentioned were contained in the songs of the various rituals in the ceremony. In every rite or song the Kúrahus described the activities of the participants and explained the meaning that everything conveyed to the Pawnee. In the actual celebration of the Hako, the people, of course, could observe and interpret the behavior and attitudes of the leader and others without the need of additional comments. No relation between the powers and man was taught without a connection with a rite of sacred object introduced into some part of the rituals.

TEACHING THROUGH SYMBOLS

The most prominent objects used in the ceremony were two feathered stems made of ash. The pith of each stick was burned out to symbolize the passage of the breath of life. One of these sticks was painted blue to represent the blue sky.

As the man paints the stick we sing. We ask, as we sing, that life be given to this symbol of the dwelling place of Tiráwa.[37]

A groove was made in the stick from one end to the other.

[35] *Ibid.,* p. 150.
[36] *Ibid.,* p. 38.
[37] *Ibid,*

We paint the groove red because the passageway through which man's breath comes and goes to give him life is red. The sun, too, is red, and the groove represents the straight path which man must travel if he would live in peace and prosper.[38]

Feathers of the brown eagle, representing the mother element and consecration to the powers, a head of a woodpecker, the purpose of which was to gain favor with the powers of the storm, feathers of the owl which could help and protect during the night, the breast, neck, and mandibles of a duck, showing their conception of an unerring guide, soft, blue feathers around the mouthpiece of the stem, pointing toward the abode of the powers, and red and white streamers, representing the sun and the moon, day and night, were all attached to the blue stem. In various ceremonies the blue stem was carried next to the people, because the brown eagle represented the mother, or gentleness and helpfulness.[39] The mother's important place in the family and in the tribe was recognized on numerous occasions in spite of the fact that the actors were men.

The other stem was similar to the one that has just been described, except that it was painted green to represent the earth and carried feathers of the white eagle, which was considered the male,[40] the father and the protector. In the rites, this stem was always carried on the outside so that it could serve as protector and not do harm or rouse contention.[41]

A third object of considerable prominence in the rites and songs was an ear of white corn. It represented the supernatural power in the earth that brought forth food for man. In the first ritual a bowl—of wood from the trees to represent a part of the living covering of Mother Earth, and round to represent the dome of the sky [42]—was provided to hold the blue paint. Standing near the paint, the Kúrahus drew the ear of corn nearer and nearer to the bowl, thus symbolizing the approach of his spirit, with the spirit of corn, toward the abode of the powers; dipping his fingers in the paint he touched the ear of corn to signify the touching of the sky by Mother Corn. He then marked four separate blue lines on the ear of corn, beginning at the tip and going about halfway toward the butt, representing the four directions or cardinal

[38] Fletcher, *The Hako, A Pawnee Religious Ceremony*, p. 38.
[39] *Ibid.*, p. 42.
[40] *Ibid.*, p. 40.
[41] *Ibid.*, p. 42.
[42] *Ibid.*, pp. 22, 44, 46.

points down which the powers descend to help man. Then paint was spread over the tip of the ear, signifying that Mother Corn had reached the abode of the powers where she received authority to lead the Hako. After this, a downy eagle feather, selected because it always moved as if breathing, was bound to a stick attached to the tip end of the ear of corn, to represent the presence of Tiráwa. Another stick, fastened to the corn and extending below the butt, was thrust into the ground to hold the ear of corn upright and keep it from touching the soil. The sticks that were used were taken from the plum tree because it was prolific. They were fastened to the corn by a braided band of hair from the head of a buffalo, in order to signify the gift of animal food and clothing.[43]

The rites also called for a braid of grass, fat from a buffalo or deer, a shell, which had once had life, to hold the paint, and the nest of an oriole. The breasts of the mother were represented by two gourd rattles, which also stood for the squash as a gift from Tiráwa.[44] These were painted to represent the dome of the sky and the four directions by which the powers came to bring help to man.

The preparation of the feathered stems, the ear of corn, and the other objects used in the Hako constituted a part of the ceremony itself. Each stage in the process was accompanied by a song, a prayer, or some significant movement. When at rest, the sacred articles were never allowed to touch the ground, but were always most reverently placed upon a wildcat skin which likewise had its symbolic meaning.[45]

The whole ceremony was symbolic. Not only the objects used but the activities themselves, when properly performed, were the means of securing special blessings from the powers above. Such relations may best be explained with the particular attitudes or virtues that are taught.

Reverence. In the first song of the first ritual, "Kusharu, sacred to rites" was addressed.[46] In the explanation by the Kúrahus, it is stated that, before a man can build a dwelling for his family, he should select a place to be made sacred, where he can be quiet and think, where he may keep the sacred objects by which he ap-

[43] *Ibid.*, pp. 22, 47.
[44] *Ibid.*
[45] *Ibid.*, pp. 23, 47.
[46] *Ibid.*, p. 33.

pealed to the powers. The Kusharu to which reference was made, means such a place. Heru, "an exclamation of reverent feeling, as when one is approaching something sacred" appears in every stanza of the first song. Many of the songs were sung to show gratitude to Tiráwa for the lesser powers that had given life to man. If, while travelling, they came to mountains or hills, they sang and remembered that the hills were made by Tiráwa.

> We ascend hills when we go away above to pray. From the top of a hill we can look over the country to see if there are enemies in sight or if any danger is near us; we can see if we are to meet friends. The hills help man, so we sing to them.[47]

In the eighth ritual, in which the Fathers fed the Children, all were urged to help, by means of reverent conduct, in the performance of the traditional rites; and before anyone could be served with food the thoughts of all were to be "turned toward Tiráwa, the father of all things." [48]

In the first ritual a priest of the Rain shrine filled a pipe for an offering of smoke to "Tiráwa, the father and giver of all things." [49] "In old times men did not smoke for pleasure as they do now, but only in religious ceremonies." Each sacred shrine of the tribe had a pipe, the proper use of which was known only to the priest.

In the ritual of the birth of Dawn the participants sang reverently as day approached, thus recognizing the fact that Tiráwa had moved upon Darkness, the Night, causing her to bring forth the Dawn.

> Mother Earth hears the call; she moves; she awakes; she arises; she feels the breath of the new-born Dawn. The leaves and the grass stir; all things move with the breath of the new day; everywhere life is renewed. This is very mysterious; we are speaking of something very sacred, although it happens every day.[50]

Throughout the ceremony, the most reverent attitude was assumed toward the sacred objects and what they represented. "I have seen manifested among the tribes not only reverence toward these sacred symbols, but an affection that was not displayed toward any other objects. Few persons ever spoke to me of them without a brightening of the eyes. 'They make us happy,' was a

[47] Fletcher, *The Hako, A Pawnee Religious Ceremony*, p. 82.
[48] *Ibid.*, p. 106.
[49] *Ibid.*, p. 48.
[50] *Ibid.*, p. 125.

common saying." [51] The journey from the lodge of the Father to the lodge of the Son sometimes required several days. The large supplies of food and valuable gifts for the Children were, of course, tempting to enemies. Yet no war party would disturb the solemn procession; "for the feathered stems are mightier than the warrior; before them he must lay down his weapon, forget his anger, and be at peace." [52]

FAMILY VIRTUES

A larger part of the whole ceremony was devoted to teachings concerning family relations than to any other aspect of life. The division of the participants into Fathers and Children implied a conception of family bonds throughout the sacred rites. One of the first duties of the father was to provide food for his children. In the lodge of the Son, therefore, the Fathers furnished food for the Children, thus symbolizing the family obligations of the male. During the remaining days of the rituals, the Father's party provided all the meals for the Son's party. It was the duty of a father not to take food himself until his children had satisfied their hunger. [53] The Son, the leader of the Children's party, was presented with suitable clothing by the chief.

Their teachings, however, did not stop with the presentation of these relationships. Specific symbols and songs were introduced to emphasize the duties of parents.

The characteristics of birds were portrayed most effectively to show how they cared for their offspring. Early in the first ritual the brown eagle was represented on the feathered stem, which was painted blue to depict the sky because, through its sacrifice to Tiráwa, this eagle had been made holy.

This stem was the first one painted because it is female and the leader. It represents the night, the moon, the north, and stands for kindness and helpfulness. It will take care of the people. It is the mother. [54]

At the same time white eagle feathers were attached to the green stem, with less power and not considered holy. "It is inclined to war, to hurt someone; it cannot lead; it must follow." In the lodge during the song, the white-eagle stem, representing the male element, was carried farther away from the people where it could

[51] *Ibid.*, p. 21.
[52] *Ibid.*, p. 302.
[53] *Ibid.*, p. 117.
[54] *Ibid.*, p. 42.

"do good by defending them and keeping away all harm." They feared it might bring war and trouble if carried nearer. The brown-eagle stem was carried next to the children "to bring them the gifts of plenty and of peace." [55]

The third song of the fifteenth ritual was explained by a man who, while walking on the prairie, saw an eagle circling above a tree. It was watching its nest.

> The white eagle, which the man saw protecting the nest, teaches all men to be brave and vigilant, to guard their children, and make safe their home. In token of this duty, the warrior father wears the white eagle feather.[56]

The duties of the warrior as guard and protector were introduced in a similar way in the song of the owl in which thanks were given to the owl for its help in the night. To the same holy man the owl appealed for a place on the feathered stem, saying:

> "Put me upon the feathered stem; for I have power to help the children. The night season is mine. I wake while others sleep. I can see in the darkness and discern coming danger. The human race must be able to care for its young during night. The warrior must be alert and ready to protect his home against prowlers in the dark. I have power to help the people so that they may not forget their young in sleep. I have power to help the people to be watchful against enemies while darkness is on the earth. I have power to help the people to keep awake and perform these ceremonies in the night as well as in the day."
>
> When the holy man awoke, he remembered what the owl had said to him, and he put the owl's feathers upon the stem, next to the duck. So the people are guided by the duck and kept awake by the owl.[57]

In the ceremonial prayer for the gift of children in the seventh ritual, Kawas, the brown eagle, as the female element, was given the lead. The watchfulness, the care, the gentleness, the diligence of the mother bird were portrayed by the movements of two doctors with eagle wings who passed to and fro in the lodge, symbolizing the duties of the mother in cleaning and purifying the home.[58]

According to the traditions of the "Song of the Woodpecker and the Turkey," there was a quarrel between the two as to which one should be the protector of the human race and have a place on the feathered stem. The woodpecker maintained that the tur-

[55] Fletcher, *The Hako, A Pawnee Religious Ceremony*, p. 42.
[56] *Ibid.*, p. 192.
[57] *Ibid.*, p. 176.
[58] *Ibid.*, p. 100.

key had many eggs but that they were hatched in places of such danger that her offspring continually decreased in number.

The woodpecker prevailed, and the turkey was deposed; for although the turkey had more children, they did not live; they were killed. Then the brown eagle was put in the turkey's place, because it was not quarrelsome, but gentle, and cared for its young, and was strong to protect them from harm.[59]

Provision for the welfare and comfort of children even before their birth, careful and constant attention during the period of helplessness, the proper guidance and direction of their activities during their early years, and joy and cheerfulness in service were all taught in the song of the bird's nest and its traditions.

THE SONG OF THE BIRD'S NEST

Words and Music

M. M. ♪ = 160.
Graphophone sound one fourth lower in pitch.
• = Pulsation of the voice.   Transcribed by Edwin S. Tracy.
No drum.

Ho-o-o-o-o! 'Ha-re, 'ha-re, i-ha-rel 'Ha-re, 'ha-re,

i-ha-rel Re wha-ka, 'ha-re, re 'ha-re, Wha-ka

'ha-re, re 'ha-re, Re wha-ka 'ha-re, re 'ha-re.

The explanation of this song by Kúrahus is so significantly educational that it is given here in full:

One day a man whose mind was open to the teaching of the powers wandered on the prairie. As he wandered, his eyes upon the ground, he spied a bird's nest hidden in the grass and arrested his feet just in time to prevent stepping on it. He paused to look at the little nest tucked away so snug and warm and noted that it held six eggs and that a peeping sound came from some of them. While he watched, one moved and soon a tiny bill pushed through the shell, uttering a shrill cry. At once, the parent birds answered, and he looked up to see where they were. They were not far off; they were flying about in search of food, chirping the while to each other, and now and then calling to the little one in the nest.

The homely scene stirred the heart and the thoughts of the man as he stood there under the clear sky, glancing upward toward the old birds and then down to the helpless young in the nest at his feet. As he looked, he thought of his people, who were so often careless and thoughtless of their children's needs, and his mind brooded over the matter. After many days

[59] *Ibid.*, pp. 173-74.

he desired to see the nest again. So he went to the place where he had found it, and there it was as safe as when he left it. But a change had taken place. It was now full to overflowing with little birds, who were stretching their wings, balancing on their little legs, and making ready to fly, while the parents with encouraging calls were coaxing the fledglings to venture forth.

"Ah!" said the man, "if my people would only learn of the birds, and, like them, care for their young and provide for their future, homes would be full and happy, and our tribe be strong and prosperous."

When this man became priest, he told the story of the bird's nest and sang its song; and so it has come down to us from the days of our fathers.[60]

In the song of the wren joy and happiness were taught as a possibility for the most humble. If the wren, the smallest of birds, could find cause to send forth its joyful trills, everyone could be happy. According to the comment of the Kúrahus:

The wren is always spoken of as the laughing bird. It is a very happy little bird, and we have stories about it. Everyone likes to hear the wren sing. This song is very old; I do not know how old, how many generations old. There are very few words in the song, but there is a story which has come down with it and which tells its meaning.

A priest went forth in the early dawn. The sky was clear. The grass and wild flowers waved in the breeze that rose as the sun threw its first beams over the earth. Birds of all kinds vied with one another as they sang their joy on that beautiful morning. The priest stood listening. Suddenly, off at one side, he heard a trill that rose higher and clearer than all the rest. He moved toward the place whence the song came that he might see what manner of bird it was that could send farther than all the others its happy, laughing notes. As he came near, he beheld a tiny brown bird with open bill, the feathers on its throat rippling with the fervor of its song. It was the wren, the smallest, the least powerful of birds, that seemed to be most glad and to pour out in ringing melody to the rising sun its delight in life.

As the priest looked, he thought: "Here is a teaching for my people. Everyone can be happy; even the most insignificant can have his song of thanks."

So he made the story of the wren and sang it; and it has been handed down from that day, a day so long ago that no man can remember the time.[61]

These songs represent a rational selection of educational material and an effective method of presenting the virtues to be taught.

THE VALUE OF THE CHILD TO THE RACE

The fifteenth ritual was devoted to secret ceremonies with songs about the flocking of the birds. The songs recited how the birds

[60] Fletcher, *The Hako, A Pawnee Religious Ceremony*, p. 170.
[61] *Ibid.*, pp. 171-72.

laid their eggs in spring, reared their young in summer, and gathered in flocks in the fall, thus symbolizing the answer to the prayer for children which was the avowed purpose of the Hako. Many of their conceptions already expressed were reviewed with significant movements and marches. In the sixteenth ritual, the Son introduced his little child who represented the continuation of life of his father. Several rites were devoted to the symbolic recognition of the child as the answer to the prayer and as the hope of the race. In his explanation the Kúrahus said:

Upon this child we are to put the signs of the promises which Mother Corn and Kawas bring, the promise of children, of increase, of long life, of plenty. The signs of these promises are put upon this little child, but they are not merely for that particular child but for its generation, that the children already born may live, grow in strength, and in their turn increase so that the family and the tribe may continue.[62]

During one song, an old man, who represented long life with many favors from the powers, touched the child's face with water. The song began with these words:

Give heed, my child, lift up your eyes, behold the one who
  is standing here;
Behold, my child! waiting here to bring the gift of strength
  to you.
Give heed, my child. Look! Water waits to bring to you the
  gift of strength.[63]

The Kúrahus explained the rite as follows:

As we sing the first stanza the old man takes up the bowl and holds it in both hands.

Water is for sustenance and the maintenance of health; it is one of the great gifts of Tiráwa atius. . . .

The water is in a bowl, shaped like the dome of the sky because water comes from Tiráwa atius. The little child is to be cleansed and prepared for its future life by the water—sustained and made strong by the water.[64]

The old man dipped his fingers in the water, made certain movements through the air, traced wet lines in the child's face to signify that the life-sustaining and cleansing power of water came from Tiráwa.

With a brush of grass the old man stroked the forehead of the child. This symbolized contact with Toharu, the "living

[62] *Ibid.*, p. 201.
[63] *Ibid.*, p. 351.
[64] *Ibid.*, p. 216.

covering of Mother Earth, the source of food and clothing," as
a gift from the powers above, which "man should always remember when he eats." [65]   The accompanying song closed with this
stanza:

> Give heed, my child, lift up your eyes, behold the one who
> has brought you food.
> Behold, my child! Food you have received, and finished is the
> task.
> Give heed, my child. Look! Grass has now here brought you
> the gift of food. [66]

The first deer or buffalo killed in a hunt belonged to Tiráwa. [67]
From its fat, ointment was made and kept in the covering of the
animal's heart, to be used in consecration ceremonies. In the
following rites, the child was anointed with this sacred ointment
and consecrated to "Tiráwa, the father above who gives life
to all things." Further touches with the sacred ointment signified that "the strength that is in every part of a man and all that
belongs to him must be consecrated to Tiráwa." [68]

Finally as a mark of the acceptance of the child by the powers,
the symbol of Tiráwa was painted on his face. Over lines that
had been made with the water, the ointment, and the red paint,
lines of blue paint were traced, forming an "arch across the
forehead and each cheek" representing the "dome of the sky, the
abode of Tiráwa atius, and a line from the middle forehead down
the ridge of the nose symbolizing the breath, of Tiráwa atius." [69]
Eagle down, taken from near the heart of the white eagle [70] and
representing the breath and life of the father, was dropped on the
head of the child, signifying recognition by Tiráwa. After the
final consecration the child was told to look into a bowl of water
and behold its face.

> The running water symbolizes the passing on of generations, one following another. The little child looks on the water and sees its own likeness, as it will see that likeness in its children and children's children. The face of Tiráwa atius is there also, giving promise that the life of the child shall go on, as the waters flow over the land. [71]

[65] Fletcher, *The Hako, A Pawnee Religious Ceremony*, p. 221.
[66] *Ibid.*, p. 352.
[67] *Ibid.*, p. 222.
[68] *Ibid.*, p. 222.
[69] *Ibid.*, p. 227.
[70] *Ibid.*, p. 237.
[71] *Ibid.*, p. 241.

There is a suggestion of a worldly immortality through the individual's own contribution to life that will continue generation after generation.

In the eighteenth ritual the child was held so that its legs touched the nest of an oriole. In this nest the Kúrahus placed some native tobacco, with bits of fat from an animal consecrated to Tiráwa. The fat represented the droppings along the path of the hunters as they brought the meat home. It represented plenty. The nest of the oriole was used because Tiráwa had taught this bird to make its nest so secure that no harm could come to it.[72] The child, as the continuation of life, typified the bird laying its eggs.

The entire act means that the clan or tribe of the Son shall increase, that there shall be peace and security, and that the land shall be covered with fatness. This is the promise of Tiráwa through the Hako.[73]

Following these rites, preparations were made for the Fathers to receive gifts from the tribe of the Children, who presented horses led by the children of the donors.[74] To honor his child, each man stopped before a stuffed figure of a man and simulated a deed of valor in an attack and told his experience. As each child came forward, a chief stroked his head with the ear of corn by which act he gave thanks for the gift and invoked a blessing upon the child. During these events two young men, one with the brown-eagle feathered stem and one with the white-eagle stem, presented a symbolic dance of thanks, while between their movements two songs were sung, both meaning: "Now fly, you eagles, as we give thanks to the Children." [75]

The twentieth ritual closed the ceremony. In the first part, the Kúrahus prayed that Tiráwa atius "would let the child grow up and become strong and find favor in its life," [76] while they repeated eight times the song:

> Breathe on him!
> Breathe on him!
> Life thou alone canst give to him.
> Long life, we pray, Oh Father, give unto him! [77]

In the second part, the sacred objects of the ceremony were presented to the Son. Expressions of appreciation and of thanks

[72] *Ibid.*, p. 244.
[73] *Ibid.*, p. 245.
[74] *Ibid.*, p. 256.
[75] *Ibid.*, p. 252.
[76] *Ibid.*, p. 258.
[77] *Ibid.*, p. 361.

were exchanged between the Fathers and the Children, after which the Children withdrew leaving the Fathers alone for the distribution of the gifts that they had received.[78]

In this way, the young Indian learned the attitudes of his people toward Tiráwa, their hope for the continuation of their race, the esteem in which he himself was held, and the responsibility that devolved upon him to contribute toward the realization of these tribal longings. As no small factors toward gaining these ends, he was taught the customs observed in the exchange of gifts and the cultivation of good will through actual participation in the practices themselves.

OTHER TRAITS

In addition to the virtues that were primarily parental, the social approval of other qualities was set forth in various ways. The value of an unerring guide was taught in the story of the song of the duck which related how the duck won its place in the ceremony. Long ago, a holy man had a dream while he was preparing the sacred objects of the Hako. The duck appeared to him, asking for a place on the feathered stem and maintaining that it had power to help the Children. Its offspring never lost their way; they travelled over water and land, finding springs and streams. They were unerring guides because they knew all the paths on the earth, on the water, or through the air. This idealization of the guide was shown by putting the duck on the handle of the stem.[79]

Provision was made in the ceremony for changing a man's name in case the warlike achievements of any member of the Son's party had been sufficiently recognized by the people. Standing under the open sky, in the presence of the people, the Kúrahus recited the ritual which described the activities and prayers connected with the custom of changing names, the achievements designated by the name to be discarded, and closed with the announcement of the new name that had been won.[80]

The recognition of fair play was shown in the division of the gifts among the members of the Father's party. Two ponies, and all the saddles, bridles, and feathers from the horses presented by the Children belonged to the Kúrahus and his aids. The rest

[78] Fletcher, *The Hako, A Pawnee Religious Ceremony*, p. 260.
[79] *Ibid.*, p. 175.
[80] *Ibid.*, pp. 272-74.

of the ponies were divided among the chiefs and the leading men on the one hand and the people on the other. To avoid the appearance of selfishness on the part of the chiefs, the Kúrahus appointed two influential men to divide the ponies into two groups. From the groups, each man selected in turn one pony at a time until the number was exhausted.[81]

Tact, shrewdness, and ingenuity were taught by the use of the wildcat skin as a covering for the sacred objects. The characteristics of the wildcat were to be imitated by the people. By it they were taught to think.

The wildcat does not make enemies by rash action. He is observant, quiet, and tactful, and he always gains his ends.[82]

We have been accustomed to concede these traits to Indian methods of warfare. In the Hako, however, such qualities were praised as the best methods for securing friends and developing friendly relationships. They were to be utilized to advance the ends of peace between the tribes.

So elaborate a ceremony conducted as a prayer for children, peace, and plenty could not but teach the desirability of peace. When it is recalled that the two parties frequently belonged to different tribes and that "between the Father and the Son and their immediate families a relationship similar to that which exists between kindred was established through this ceremony," [83] it can scarcely be denied that the Hako must have stimulated more cordial feelings between different groups.

COMPARISON WITH OTHER RELIGIOUS CEREMONIES

The Hako as a ceremony was not alone in maintaining a religious spirit throughout. Practically every society had provision for more or less elaborate rituals by which the visions or the aid of the supernatural powers were invoked. Hunting societies, before starting out for game, and war parties, as an essential feature of their preparation, often made sacrifices and offered prayers to the powers in order to secure supernatural help in accomplishing their purposes. In a sense, the whole of many of the sun dances contributed toward a vision sought by the candidates in relation to their aims or vows. Many of these ceremonies, however, did not show clearly their specific teaching values.

[81] *Ibid.*, p. 260.
[82] *Ibid.*, pp. 23, 47.
[83] *Ibid.*, p. 49.

The Oglala, however, performed a ceremony with so many traits in common with the Hako that we are led to believe it must have originated with the latter. They called it the Hunka.[84] By its rites, two persons adopted the Hunka relationship which bound each one to the other by "ties of fidelity stronger than friendship, brotherhood, or family." When one of the two was much older than the other, the relationship was much like that of parent and child. While there was no organization or society, those for whom the ceremony had been performed were called Hunkayapi; and the relationship among these individuals was called Hunkaya, a term which showed a feeling of fellowship beyond the two who were Hunka to each other.

Dr. Walker says it is probable that at first there was little ceremony beyond an agreement between two persons. Even at the time of his investigation, the Hunka rites ranged "from a very simple affair to an elaborate event."

The wands that were used, the rattles, the ear of corn, the conductor, and the Hunka relationship show a striking similarity to the feathered stems,[85] the rattles, the corn, the Conductor, and the relation between the Father and the Son in the Hako. Many of the rites also give strong evidences of borrowed features. The fact that the ear of corn was treated much the same way as in the Hako suggests that the ceremony came from the Pawnee who depended more on corn than did the northern tribes.

Reverence was taught in a prayer at the beginning of the ceremony. Fidelity, truthfulness, bravery, industry, generosity, and revenge were all presented as desirable qualities, but in the Hunka the appeal made to individual or selfish motives fell far short of the broad social purposes of the Hako.

THE DREAMERS

In his report on the Menomini Indians, Dr. Hoffman states that in three localities, near Keshena, Wisconsin, meetings were held for promulgating the doctrines of a society called "The Dreamers," which became known to the Menomini in 1880 "through the Potawatomi of the Prairie, or those living in Indian territory and Kansas." [86] They had their ceremonial smoke, their

[84] Walker, *The Sun Dance and Other Ceremonies of the Oglala Division of the Teton Dakota*, pp. 122-32.
[85] *Ibid.*, p. 124.
[86] Hoffman, *Fourteenth Annual Report of the Bureau of American Ethnology*, p. 157.

drum, and their dances with addresses by braves. The Menomini maintained that the dance of "The Dreamers" was given
them to preserve a "purer ritual and religious observance."

Metchikeni, a Dreamer, explained the society's origin and purpose to Reverend Clay MacCauley, a census official, who attended
a meeting about 1880.[87] Apparently they had encountered opposi-
tion. He claimed that they meant no ill but wanted to be allowed
to continue their dances. They attributed their origin to the visions
of a woman who had been drowned and brought back to life by
the Great Spirit who told her:

> Go at once to your people and tell them to stop their war and to be-
> come friends with one another and with the white man. . . . And when
> you speak, say always these things: "You are all children of one Father,
> and are brothers. You must live in peace with one another. You must
> not drink intoxicating drink. You must always speak the truth. If you
> are struck, you must count the blow as nothing and not strike back again."
> Do these things, and all Indians and white men will soon be prosperous
> and at peace and happy. You will all have one heart. . . . You saw a
> sick girl carried into our holy place. She was carried there that there
> we might pray to the Great Spirit to make her well. We have no medicine
> dance. We hope with our dance to break up, by and by, the old medicine
> dance and all such things. So we teach. . . .[88]

In explaining the significance of the rituals which MacCauley
had witnessed, he said:

> We lifted our hands to the sky; that was for prayer. We held out our
> hands, palms upward; that was to receive the answers to our prayers.
> We scattered from our hands to the ground; that was to show that we
> give what we receive. You saw us all give presents to one another; that
> was to show that we are brothers, and that brothers must help brothers. . . .
> If I had a flag of my own, I should want to have painted on it a picture
> of a plow and over that my totem, the eagle. This flag I should like to
> see always waving over our dance. I want all my children to go to school
> to learn just what white men know. . . . We are doing the best we can.[89]

MacCauley observed that the Dreamers were "evidently thoroughly, even fanatically in earnest." He attributed their organization to a "strange admixture of pagan ritual, monolatory, or degenerate Christian theology and Christian ethics." [90]

The degenerate ethics are not so apparent after all. The Dreamers taught generosity, coöperation, the fatherhood of God, and the

[87] *Ibid.*, p. 160.
[88] *Ibid.*, p. 160.
[89] *Ibid.*, p. 161.
[90] *Ibid.*

universal brotherhood of man.   In these ideals the society assumed
a place by the side of the Hako, ranking above any other organization of its kind.

The Teachings of the Hako

While the Hako was religious throughout, it contained no suggestion of a life after death and hence no idea of punishment in
the next world.   Ritualistic procedure and life along a straight
and narrow path were taught as the means of securing aid from
the powers.   The ceremony omitted the fantastic accounts of the
creation of the world and the origin of man that were found even
among the myths of the Pawnee.   The Hako made no appeal
to magic and invoked no supernatural aid to accomplish the selfish
ends of any individual.   As a prayer for children, peace, and
plenty, it did not stop with the expression of a yearning desire
that might be realized through self-torture or assured through
ceremonial procedure alone.   Without neglecting fecundity as a
factor in the perpetuation of, the race, its moving ideal was the
proper nurture and conservation of the child trained to share the
fondest hopes of the tribe.   In order to gain the object of their
supplications, the Pawnee were taught that they should observe
the fundamental laws of life in the protection and care of offspring.   With the establishment of the relation between the Father
and the Son and the promotion of peace between the tribes as a
setting, the underlying purpose of the Hako became education,
or the transmission of certain ideals or attitudes to affect the life
and conduct of all the people.

There are internal evidences to indicate that the same fundamental educational purpose determined the growth and development of the Hako.   In the midst of the suggestive solitude of
the far-reaching prairies, certain men with their minds especially
open to the teachings of the powers, claimed, in a reverent spirit,
that they were inspired to see the teachings of the songs of the
eagles, of the bird's nest, and of the wren.

It should be noted, also, that the educational values in these
teachings were transmitted more upon the basis of their own in-
herent worth than upon the authority of a law-giver.   With an
open mind, the seer saw in nature great truths that carried convic-
tion with them.   There were no reasons for the family virtues
that were taught except their service to the group.

With minds keenly alert to the silent influences of their environment, these sons of the Plains saw back of all the works of nature one mighty power, Tiráwa atius, the Maker of All. The Winds, the Sun, the Earth, Vegetation, and Water were gifts from this Father of All. Through them he had sent to men the breath of life, health, vitality, strength, food, and clothing. In reverence and gratitude, they recognized him as the life-sustaining power to whom they could appeal in time of need.

Likewise, with a feeling of sympathetic kinship for birds and animals, they saw their own vital problems reflected in the life that surrounded them. From situations found in their environment, they selected relationships by which to teach the ideals of a gentle, helpful, and solicitous mother and a strong, watchful, and courageous father. On the other hand, the Hako neglected the treatment of many virtues taught in other ceremonies of the Plains and highly esteemed by the Pawnee themselves. In morals, as in theology, it seemed to endeavor to select certain fundamentals and to teach them well.

The ideas and virtues were not presented in abstract discourses or as specific rules of conduct. In an elaborate scheme of poetic symbolism, the various conceptions were portrayed through objects, colors, dances, rites, and songs, each one of which teemed with meanings for the people who witnessed the ceremony. Thus, by the use of symbols and significant rites and songs, the Hako taught principles and attitudes rather than a detailed code of conventional morality.

There is implied in many of the teachings a conception of the ideal of unselfish service. The duck, the owl, and the woodpecker all asked for a place on the feathered stem so that they might help the human race by their own particular qualities. All the lesser powers were looked upon as gifts from Tiráwa for the good of man. The parental duties portrayed in the rituals represented individual obligations to strive for the good of the people. Even the child was taught that, as he looked into running water, the face he saw represented his contribution to the great onward-flowing stream of human life.

In the teaching of these qualities, the proper emotional attitudes were not neglected. Songs, dances, feasts, and presents contributed to keep the people joyous and happy. They were deeply moved in reverent prayer at times, and on other occasions they shouted with joy at the exchange of gifts and the promised blessings from the Hako.

A question may be raised concerning the extent that the ideals of the Hako prevailed among the Indians. Dunbar observed that parents welcomed children and were very fond of them. Some of the chiefs were genuine fathers to their people. Among Pawnee hero stories, Comanche Chief (the Peace Maker), Lone Chief, and Little Warrior, famous for their war records, were also highly esteemed for their success in making peace with hostile tribes.[91]

This account would be incomplete without some comment on the Kúrahus, the leader of the whole ceremony. As an apprentice under special instruction, he had had to pay for his knowledge concerning the rites and songs of the Hako. Years had been spent in prayerful study of its rituals and their meanings so that they might be preserved as their fathers had taught them. To insure that his knowledge would be appreciated, the Kúrahus was under obligations to charge for teaching how to conduct the Hako ceremony. From the gifts presented by the Children, two ponies as a rule went to the leader. He was a primitive teacher paid for his services.

Tahirussawichi, the Kúrahus who made the record for Miss Fletcher, did not seem to have mercenary motives in his work. Past seventy years of age, with the scars of battle on his forehead, and standing near the end of a career that had been devoted largely to the preservation of the spiritual inheritance of his people, this reverent worshiper of Tiráwa atius, the Maker of All, was stirred by the deepest emotions as he prayed for the child at the close of the rituals. And after he had finished the task of his contribution to the first written record of the songs, rituals, and prayers that expressed the cherished longings of his people in the past, he delivered a touching farewell in this brief meditation:

When I think of all the people of my own tribe who have died during my lifetime and then of those of other tribes that have fallen by our hands, they are so many they make a vast cover over Mother Earth. I once walked with those prostrate forms. I did not fall but I passed on, wounded sometimes but not to death, until I am here to-day doing this thing, singing these sacred songs into that great pipe (the graphophone) and telling of these ancient rites of my people. It must be that I have been preserved for this purpose, otherwise I should be lying back there among the dead.[92]

91 Grinnell, *op. cit.*, pp. 25-66, 79-82.
92 Fletcher, *op. cit.*, p. 278.

CHAPTER VI

CHARACTERISTICS OF INDIAN MORALITY AND EDUCATION

The Indians of North America lived in an atmosphere surcharged with a consciousness of the supernatural powers. On the fertile prairies of the Central Plains, on the islands and the coast of the distant Pacific, on the elevated mesas, or in the rich valleys of the picturesque Southwest, the cultivated fear of, and deference to, the unseen spirits pervaded their daily activities, their fascinating hunt, and their engrossing warfare. Out of this attitude, and no doubt profiting by it, developed their first professional class—men who devoted themselves to the study and explanation of the mystifying events of life in terms of the spirit world.

When the Indians had once accepted the premise that the natural phenomena of life were controlled by unseen spirits with personal qualities, the stimulus to search for other methods of explanation was removed. Indian priests, shamans, or medicine men, therefore, elaborated comprehensive theories prescribing innumerable forms to be followed in overcoming the potency, avoiding the anger, appeasing the wrath, or securing the aid of jealous, supernatural beings.

Most of the conventional forms and rites taught by the priesthood were based on supernatural demands or sanctions and had little or no rational ethical bearing. On the other hand, hunters and warriors, by the very nature of the situations that confronted them, were compelled to employ methods related in no small degree to actual and immediate causes and effects. Action based on false premises meant the escape of the wild game or possibly the death of the warrior at the hands of the enemy. Thus the mental operations of the Indians in meeting the demands of experience were much more reliable than their hypothetical reasoning concerning the workings of spirits.

The ethical morality of the Indians did not grow out of their

95

theories about spirits but originated from their immediate social experiences and from their observation of the natural environment. In other words, they developed a rational morality based on its connection with actual human needs and social relationships. The ideal aims of Indian education in ethical morality, then, were clear and specific, because they were conceived as means for the attainment of definite human ends.

ETHICAL AIMS OF EDUCATION

The Indian man was taught to provide food for his family and to be generous and brotherly in his group. He was trained to be a guide, familiar with path and stream, as trustworthy as the unerring duck. He was urged to be a watchman as alert and as vigilant as the sleepless owl. In accomplishing his purposes, he was told to be a thinker as cautious and tactful as the wildcat in the forest. He was taught to keep his word and to shed his own blood to demonstrate the fulfillment of his vows. He was inured to hardships and trained to endure with fortitude the pain and suffering incident to his precarious life. He was taught to be loyal to his friend, even unto death. He was taught to nurture and honor a burning desire for revenge in return for injuries done by the enemy. Above all, in defence of his family and his tribe, he was trained to be as valiant and courageous, and as cruel and relentless, as the white-eagle father in the defense of his offspring.

The Indian woman was taught to be industrious like the spider, wise and silent like the turtle, and cheerful like the lark. In the care of her family, her ideal was to be provident, helpful, and solicitous like the brown-eagle mother. Her duties were portrayed to her through the eagle's nest, safe from all harm, filled with growing birds, or through the ingenious home of the oriole, comfortable and free from danger. The Buffalo Ceremony shows unusually well the ideal aims conceived for the girl. As the rewards of industry, chastity, 'and fidelity, her teacher envisaged for her a brave man as a husband and protector, happy growing children, an abundance of food, and a permanent fire in an attractive tipi. As the wages of laziness and lewdness, he portrayed for her a vision of a coyote, a homeless, loafing vagabond, an old and ragged robe, worn moccasins without color, and a "voice in mourning."

Loyalty to the group and devotion to those activities directly related to the protection, preservation, and happiness of its members constituted the fundamental ideals that Indian education sought to instill in the minds of all. They constantly emphasized the importance of actual achievement. In so doing, consciously or unconsciously, they encouraged no small degree of individuality.

The Agencies and Means of Moral Education

The parent, the godfather, the story-teller, the tutor, the orator, and the conductor of public ceremonies were undoubtedly conscious of the fact that they were transmitting ethical ideas and were endeavoring to make those ideas prevail. Childhood play, the daily happenings of the village, adult pursuits, the search for wild game, warfare and its influences, puberty rites, the activities of special societies and public ceremonies all served to furnish occasions for the arousal of moral sentiments and the direction of attention to the qualities of character most highly prized by the tribe.

Outside of Mexico, among the Indians studied, there were practically no written records to guide the parent, the story-teller and the ceremonial teacher or to aid in the preservation of the ideas which they taught. Sometimes, through gifts from appreciative hearers, the story-teller was encouraged to specialize in the traditions of his people. However, the great preserver of tribal lore was the conductor of religious ceremonies. By the constant use of symbols, the ideas conveyed and the rites performed in ceremonies were held together more or less permanently. A few men, some through a hereditary priestly office, connected with a particular society or sacred bundle, and some through special inclination, as in the Hako and the sun dance, were stimulated by tribal honors and material rewards to devote their entire lives to the study of the songs, dances, rituals, and teachings of different ceremonies. Such men could be called the special guardians of learning and the teachers of the people.

Methods of Teaching Ethical Ideas

An understanding of Indian methods of teaching morals can be made clear through a statement of the conclusions reached by Todd in his study of *The Primitive Family as an Educational Agency*, in which he included a brief discussion of various factors outside the family. He found the methods of primitive education to be memory, imitation, exhortation, story-telling, drill, and control through magic or the fear of the supernatural. He asserts that "primitive society left out almost entirely the development of the habit of thinking." In speaking of the teaching of morals, he says:

To be sure, such moral instruction is largely unethical and consists rather in the *what*, the content of the social code, and only rarely the *why*. Unreasoned acquiescence is the most becoming attitude in savage discipline. If it ever occurs to the learner to question, more *what* is invented to explain the difficulty.[1]

Such conclusions harmonize in part with the facts that have been presented concerning Indian education, but in some important respects they fail to agree with observations that are clearly justified by the evidence gathered in these chapters.

Imitation, exhortation, and story-telling as educational methods of the Indians are not to be questioned. Training might be a better term than drill, as it emphasizes the achievement rather than exercise in the process, for the method of learning followed by the average individual. While all tradition had to be preserved through memory, the memoriter method as such was probably not used much except by the priestly guardians of sacred-bundle rituals or by the conductor of public ceremonies.

On the subject of thinking, however, Todd greatly minimizes the practice of encouraging the use of reason. His conclusion was due no doubt to the lack of ethical teachings in much of the data which he used. Under the moral, he placed "custom, tradition, and religion,"[2] and his conclusion will hold if ethical morality is omitted. The Indians, however, did not leave ethical ideas out of their teachings.

Instead of neglecting rational ethical ideals, as Todd suggests, the Indians rather built up their ethical notions around legitimate reasons for the practices which they approved. From the social experience of the individual and from his observations of people, birds, and animals, Indian teachers pointed out the good results of ethical conduct and the distressing outcome of wrongdoing. In fact, they endeavored in many ways to stimulate the individual to reflect on the ideas which they were imparting. Through the use of objects full of symbolic meaning, through the recall or

[1] Todd, *The Primitive Family as an Educational Agency,* p. 171.
[2] *Ibid.,* p. 146.

the presentation of life experiences, and through honors bestowed on those who practiced the virtues, the individual was stimulated by objective situations, concerning the fundamental significance of which there could be no doubt.

The Indians taught many ethical ideas under the emotional conditions that were most favorable for making desirable impressions. At tribal reunions, at feasts and joyous celebrations, the virtues were exhibited and honored as a part of the whole group interest and activity. The individual was not made conscious of the fact that his ideals were being formulated in harmony with those of the tribe. To a certain extent, the Indian youth was left free to decide whether he would seek the approval of his fellow tribesmen. The normal individual simply absorbed the spirit of his people.

Not only was the youth given an understanding of the virtues in their connection with life, but his own desire to secure the rewards of the virtues was aroused. Direct instruction and exhortation reinforced and helped to keep alive the desire to win social approval through the achievement honored by the tribe.

INDIAN LIFE AND EDUCATION

It should not be inferred that all Indians lived up to the ideals which were taught in the tribe. Since there existed a certain degree of freedom in ethical morality, ethical teachings were not enforced as uniformly as were the customs and conventional practices supported by supernatural sanction. While practical reasoning and social ideals were controlling factors in the conduct of some, the behavior of others was determined largely by a conventional code which relied on the fear of unseen spirits for the observance of its details. In the Southwest, fear of the supernatural was definitely employed in teaching the social virtues, but in most of the tribes of North America ethical values were based on human relationships.

With these conditions in mind, and with the admission of some repetition of ideas already expressed, the following may be considered the broad characteristics of Indian education:

1. In individual instruction, in public teaching, and in their various types of training, the Indians showed that they based their ethical ideas on social experience and considered learning, through social experience and observation, the best method for the development of the attitudes and ideals which they cherished.

2. The Indians always tended to convey their ethical ideals in terms of concrete, objective results. Even in their direct moral instruction, they repeatedly utilized a story with its complex setting or recalled the learner's observations and experiences to express their moral ideas through life situations. It seemed to be their conscious purpose to make the specific rewards of the virtues so attractive and the lack of them so annoying that the individual would exert every effort to realize the ideals of his tribe. In other words, their teaching of ethical ideas was weighted with reasons why the individual should strive to embody the virtues in his life. In such precedure they worked directly on the original nature of the child. They brought into play the very springs of human action, the native impulses, the growing desires, and the deepest emotions of the individual.

3. In the most effective influences which tended to arouse the desire for the realization of their ideals, the Indians used few words and little exhortation. They developed an atmosphere from which escape was almost impossible. In the sun dance and in military societies, they presented objective situations to which individuals were ready to respond, even if the effort demanded the prolonged endurance of pain and the shedding of their own blood. It was clearly demonstrated that there were scarcely any limits to what the Indians would undertake toward the attainment of specific ends when social stimulation was properly presented.

The direct contact of their education with the actual pursuits and activities of adults made possible an emphasis on achievement and ethical conduct that is difficult to provide in more complex situations. Their practices illustrate a principle stated so well by Dewey:

> Taste, appreciation, and effort always spring from some objective situation. They have objective support. . . . Taste and desire represent a prior objective fact recurring in action to secure perpetuation and extension.[3]

The whole environment of the Indians contributed toward the development of their taste for the activities through which their ideals were realized and the increase of their appreciation of the rewards offered. It stimulated their most strenuous efforts by keeping their eyes fixed on ethical goals to be reached or social results to be secured.

[3] Dewey, *Human Nature and Conduct*, p. 22.

BIBLIOGRAPHY

CURTIS, EDWARD S. The North American Indian, Vol. IV. Cambridge University Press, Cambridge, 1909.

DORSEY, GEORGE A. The Cheyenne. Field Columbian Museum, Anthropological Series, Vol. II, Chicago, 1905.

DORSEY, GEORGE A. The Pawnee. Mythology. Washington, 1906.

DORSEY, GEORGE A. The Sun Dance, Field Columbian Museum, Anthropological Series, Vol. IX, No. 2. Chicago, 1905.

DORSEY, GEORGE A. Traditions of the Skidi Pawnee. Memoirs of the American Folk Lore Society, Vol. VIII. Boston and New York, 1904.

DORSEY, GEORGE A. and KROEBER, A. L. Traditions of the Arapaho, Field Columbian Museum, Anthropological Series, Vol. V. Chicago, 1903.

DUNBAR, JOHN B. The Pawnee Indians; Their History and Ethnology. Magazine of American History, Vols. IV and V. 1880.

EASTMAN, CHARLES A. Indian Boyhood. McClure, Phillips & Co., New York, 1902.

FLETCHER, ALICE C. The Hako, A Pawnee Religious Ceremony. Twenty-second Annual Report, Bureau of American Ethnology, Part II. Washington, D. C., 1904.

GODDARD, PLINY E. Dancing Societies of the Sarsi Indians. Anthropological Papers, American Museum of Natural History, Vol. XI, Part V. New York, 1914.

GODDARD, PLINY E. Indians of the Southwest. Handbook Series, American Museum of Natural History, No. 2. New York, 1921.

GODDARD, PLINY E. Notes on the Sun Dance of the Cree in Alberta. Anthropological Papers, American Museum of Natural History, Vol. XVI, Part IV, pp. 299-310. New York, 1919.

GODDARD, PLINY E. Notes on the Sun Dance of the Sarsi, Anthropological Papers, American Museum of Natural History, Vol. XVI, Part IV, pp. 273-82. New York, 1919.

GRINNELL, GEORGE BIRD. Pawnee Hero Stories and Folk Tales. New York, 1889.

Handbook of American Indians, Vols. I and II. Government Printing Office, Washington, 1907 and 1910.

HOFFMAN, WALTER J. Midewiwin or Grand Medicine Society of the Ojibway, Seventh Annual Report, Bureau of American Ethnology. Washington, D. C., 1891.

HOFFMAN, WALTER J. The Menomini Indians, Fourteenth Annual Report, Bureau of American Ethnology, Part I. Washington, D. C., 1897.

KROEBER, ALFRED L. American Culture and the Northwest Coast. American Anthropologist, N. S., Vol. XXV, pp. 1-20, 1923.

KROEBER, ALFRED L. The Arapaho. Bulletin American Museum of Natural History, Vol. XVIII, pp. 279-454. New York, 1907.

LOWIE, ROBERT H. Military Societies of the Crow Indians. Anthropological Papers, American Museum of Natural History, Vol. XI, Part III. New York, 1913.

LOWIE, ROBERT H. Societies of the Arikara Indians. Anthropological Papers, American Museum of Natural History, Vol. XI, Part VIII. New York, 1915.

LOWIE, ROBERT H. Societies of the Crow, Hidasta, and Mandan Indians. Anthropological Papers, American Museum of Natural History, Vol. XI, Part III. New York, 1913.

LOWIE, ROBERT H. Sun Dance of the Shoshoni, Ute, and Hidatsa. Anthropological Papers, American Museum of Natural History, Vol. I, Part V. New York, 1919.

LOWIE, ROBERT H. The Sun Dance of the Crow Indians. Anthropological Papers, American Museum of Natural History, Vol. XVI, Part I. New York, 1919.

MURIE, JAMES R. Pawnee Indian Societies. Anthropological Papers, American Museum of Natural History, Vol. XI, Part VII. New York, 1914.

PAGET, AMELIA M. The People of the Plains. Toronto, 1909.

POWELL, J. W. Indian Linguistic Families of America North of Mexico. Seventh Annual Report, Bureau of American Ethnology. Washington, D. C., 1891.

RUSSELL, FRANK. The Pima Indians. Twenty-sixth Annual Report, Bureau of American Ethnology, pp. 3-389. Washington, D. C., 1908.

SAHAGUN, BERNARDINO DE. Histoire Générale des Choses de la Nouvelle-Espagne. (Translated and edited by D. Jourdanet and Rémi Siméon.) Paris, 1880.

SKINNER, ALANSON. Notes on the Sun Dance of the Sisseton Dakota, Anthropological Papers, American Museum of Natural History, Vol. XVI, Part IV, pp. 381-85. New York, 1919.

SKINNER, ALANSON. The Sun Dance of the Plains—Cree. Anthropological Papers, American Museum of Natural History, Vol. XVI, Part IV, pp. 285-93. New York, 1919.

SKINNER, ALANSON. The Sun Dance of the Plains—Ojibway. Anthropological Papers, American Museum of Natural History, Vol. XVI, Part IV, pp. 311-15. New York, 1919.

SPENCER, FRANK C. Education of the Pueblo Child. Columbia University, New York, 1899.

SPIER, LESLIE. Notes on the Kiowa Sun Dance. Anthropological Papers, American Museum of Natural History, Vol. XVI, Part VI. New York, 1921.

SPIER, LESLIE. The Sun Dance of the Plains Indians: Its Development and Diffusion. Anthropological Papers, American Museum of Natural History, Vol. XVI, Part VII. New York, 1921.

SPINDEN, H. J. Ancient Civilization of Mexico and Central America.

Handbook Series, American Museum of Natural History, No. 3. New York, 1917.

STEVENSON, MATILDE COXE. The Religious Life of the Zuñi Child. Fifth Annual Report, Bureau of American Ethnology, pp. 533-55. Washington, D. C., 1887.

STEVENSON, MATILDE COXE. The Zuñi Indians. Twenty-third Annual Report, Bureau of American Ethnology. Washington, D. C., 1904.

SWANTON, JOHN R. Tlingit Myths and Texts. Bulletin 39, Bureau of American Ethnology. Washington, D. C., 1909.

SWANTON, JOHN R. Social Condition, Beliefs, and Linguistic Relationship of the Tlingit Indians. Twenty-sixth Annual Report, Bureau of American Ethnology, pp. 391-485. Washington, D. C., 1908.

WALKER, J. R. T. The Sun Dance and Other Ceremonies of the Oglala Division of the Teton Dakota. Anthropological Papers, American Museum of Natural History, Vol. XVI, Part II. New York, 1917.

WALLIS, W. D. The Sun Dance of the Canadian Dakota. Anthropological Papers, American Museum of Natural History, Vol. XVI, Part IV, pp. 317-80. New York, 1919.

WISSLER, CLARK. North American Indians of the Plains. Handbook Series, American Museum of Natural History, No. 1. New York, 1920.

WISSLER, CLARK. Societies and Ceremonial Associations in the Oglala Division of the Teton-Dakota. Anthropological Papers, American Museum of Natural History, Vol. XI, Part I. New York, 1912.

WISSLER, CLARK. Societies and Dance Associations of the Blackfoot Indians. Anthropological Papers, American Museum of Natural History, Vol. XI, Part IV. New York, 1913.

WISSLER, CLARK. Societies of the Plains Indians. Anthropological Papers, American Museum of Natural History, Vol. XI, Introduction. New York, 1916.

WISSLER, CLARK. The American Indian. Oxford University Press, New York, 1922.

WISSLER, CLARK. The Sun Dance of the Blackfoot Indians. Anthropological Papers, American Museum of Natural History, Vol. XVI, Part III. New York, 1918.

SECONDARY SOURCES

Most of the following works present broad surveys of primitive education. Some of them refer more to primitive culture in general. They have been valuable as guides in the selection and arrangement of facts rather than as sources of specific data in the particular field of moral education among the North American Indians.

BARNES, EARL and MARY S. Education among the Aztecs. Studies in Education, Leland Stanford, Jr., University, Vol. I, pp. 73-80. 1896.

BOSANQUET, HELEN. The Family. Macmillan & Co., limited, London, 1906.

BRINTON, DANIEL G. The Basis of Social Relations. Livingston Farrand, New York and London, 1906.

CHRISMAN, OSCAR. The Historical Child, Chap. I. Richard G. Badger, Boston, 1920.

DAVIDSON, THOMAS. History of Education. Charles Scribner's Sons, New York, 1900.

DEWEY, JOHN. Human Nature and Conduct. Henry Holt & Co., New York, 1922.

FLETCHER, ALICE C. Indian Education and Civilization. Bureau of Education, Washington, D. C., 1888.

GOODSELL, WILLESTINE. History of the Family as a Social and Educational Institution, Chap. I. The Macmillan Co., New York, 1919.

GRAVES, FRANK P. History of Education before the Middle Ages, Chap. II. Macmillan, New York, 1909.

MONROE, PAUL. Textbook in the History of Education. The Macmillan Co., New York, 1920.

STARR, F. Some First Steps in Human Progress. Chautauqua, New York, 1901.

TODD, ARTHUR J. The Primitive Family as an Educational Agency. G. P. Putnam's Sons, New York and London, 1913.

TYLOR, E. B. Anthropology. London, 1889.

TYLOR, E. B. Primitive Culture, Vol. I. Brentano's, New York, 1920.

WEBSTER, HUTTON. Primitive Secret Societies. The Macmillan Co., New York, 1908.